THEOCRACIES

ABDO
Publishing Company

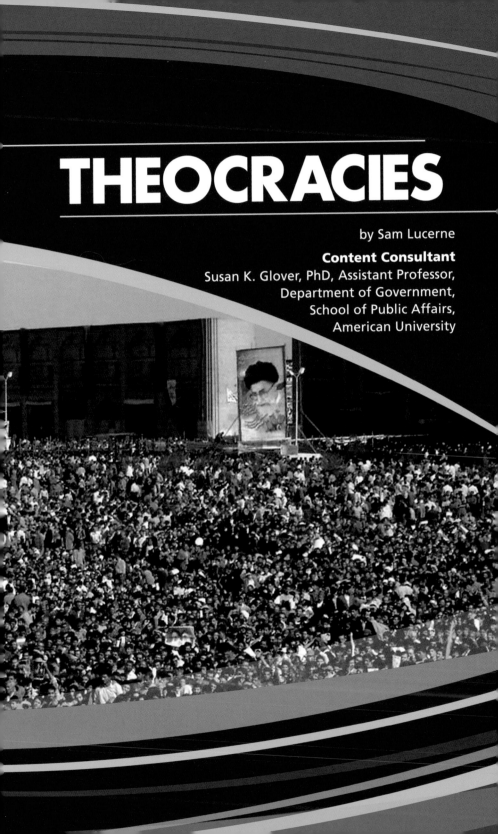

THEOCRACIES

by Sam Lucerne

Content Consultant
Susan K. Glover, PhD, Assistant Professor,
Department of Government,
School of Public Affairs,
American University

CREDITS

Published by ABDO Publishing Company, 8000 West 78th Street, Edina, Minnesota 55439. Copyright © 2011 by Abdo Consulting Group, Inc. International copyrights reserved in all countries. No part of this book may be reproduced in any form without written permission from the publisher. The Essential Library™ is a trademark and logo of ABDO Publishing Company.

Printed in the United States of America,
North Mankato, Minnesota
112010
012011

 THIS BOOK CONTAINS AT LEAST 10% RECYCLED MATERIALS.

Editor: Holly Saari
Copy Editor: David Johnstone
Interior Design and Production: Becky Daum
Cover Design: Becky Daum

Photo Credits: AP Images, cover, 2, 3, 108; Library of Congress, 9, 136; Thomas Gold Appleton/Library of Congress, 12; Georgios Kollidas/Fotolia, 21; W.B. Carson/Library of Congress, 31; Manuel Velasco/iStockphoto, 33; Michael Rahel/ Shutterstock Images, 37; Bernhard Richter/iStockphoto, 42; Hasan Sarbakhshian/AP Images, 45; iStockphoto, 49, 83, 95; Antoine Beyeler/iStockphoto, 55; C. Brothers/Library of Congress, 59; Kirsty Wigglesworth/AP Images, 63; Kamran Jebreili/AP Images, 67, 99; Arshia Kiani/AP Images, 74; Prakash Hatvalne/AP Images, 77; Floriano Rescigno/iStockphoto, 81; Robert Ellis/iStockphoto, 93; Bain News Service/Library of Congress, 103; Shutterstock Images, 113; Pier Paolo Cito/AP Images, 115; Ivan Sekretarev/AP Images, 119; Altaf Qadri/AP Images, 128; Rich Koele/Shutterstock Images, 131

Library of Congress Cataloging-in-Publication Data
Lucerne, Sam, 1968-
  Theocracies / by Sam Lucerne.
      p. cm. -- (Exploring world governments)
  Includes bibliographical references.
  ISBN 978-1-61714-794-4
  1. Theocracy. I. Title.
  JC372.L83 2011
  321'.5--dc22
                                    2010045857

Table of Contents

INTRODUCTION

What Is Government?

In the earliest, simplest societies, government as we know it did not exist. Family or tribal elders made decisions, and their powers were limited. As civilizations grew, governments developed to organize societies and to protect them from outside threats. As societies have grown in complexity, so have the governments that organize them. In this way, organizing society has led to massive bureaucracies with many offices and roles.

As of 2010, there were more than 190 countries, each with its own government. Two governments may look very similar on paper even though political life inside those countries varies greatly. Every government is different because it is influenced by its country's history, culture, economics, geography, and even psychology.

Still, governments share some main roles. Today, a main function of governments is to protect citizens from outside threats. This has evolved into the vast arena of international relations, including military alliances and trade agreements. Governments also organize power in a society. However, how power is acquired—through elections, heredity, or force—varies, as does who exercises it—one person, a few, or many.

Ideally, governments balance the rights of individuals against the needs of the whole society. But who defines those needs? Is it leaders chosen by universal suffrage, or is it a single dictator who assumed power through force? How are individual rights protected? The answers to these questions distinguish one form of government from another.

Another role of government is preserving internal order—that is, order as defined by those in power. While keeping order might mean prosecuting violent criminals in a democracy, in a dictatorship, it could mean prosecuting dissenters. Governments also look out for the welfare of their citizens. All modern governments provide some form of social services, ranging from education to housing to health care.

Governments are often involved in their national economies. Involvement can run the full spectrum—from completely planning the economy to merely levying taxes and allowing a free market to operate. Governments also regulate the private lives of citizens—from issuing marriage licenses in a democracy to enforcing specific styles of dress in a theocracy.

While all governments have some characteristics in common, the world's governments take many forms and make decisions differently. How does a government decide what individual rights to give its citizens? How are laws enforced? What happens when laws are broken? The answers to such questions depend on the political system at hand. ⌘

Theocracy in the New World

When early European settlers came to America, they were often seeking adventure, territory, and opportunity. But many of those coming to the New World were seeking something else, too—the freedom to practice religion as they chose. During that time period, England was ruled by a monarchy, a system of government that was ruled by a king. Although religion was not the law of the land, the king was closely tied to the Church of England. The ruler of the church, the archbishop, enforced a strict interpretation of religion, and the king

An 1854 wood engraving commemorated John Winthrop, the first governor of the Massachusetts Bay Colony.

GOV. JOHN WINTHROP.

passed down these religious rules to his subjects. In the seventeenth century, King Charles sat on the throne of England, and William Laud served as the archbishop of Canterbury. Laud was a forceful figure with little tolerance for dissenters like the Puritans, a group who wanted to rid the Church of England of Catholic influences.

At the time, England's politics were in turmoil, and religious persecution toward Puritans increased. The situation in England became intolerable for them. When a group of Puritans learned of a new land grant in America in the area that is now Massachusetts, they decided to take advantage of the opportunity and create a colony where they could practice their religion freely. Unlike charter agreements that came before it, this new charter allowed the leader of the territory to be located in the New World rather than in England. In essence, this meant that the Puritans could choose their own form of government and rule themselves in North America.

The first Puritans arrived in Massachusetts in 1630 and set up the colony as a place where they could practice their religion freely. Unlike adventurers who had come to America in the ten years prior, the colonists of the Massachusetts Bay Colony brought wealth and education. Many of them had held prominent positions in England. One of the primary founders, John Winthrop, was the first governor of the Massachusetts Bay Colony. Over the next ten years, the Puritans in England began a massive exodus to America, where many of them became members of the first theocratic colony in the New World, the Massachusetts Bay Colony.

A Theocratic Colony

A theocratic government defers to the will of God or another deity in ruling a society. For the Puritans, this meant the opportunity to practice their religion freely without fear of imprisonment or torture. Wealth and education were not the only factors that set apart the Massachusetts Bay Colony from its neighbors. All settlers to the New World were Pilgrims, but the term Puritan is a religious designation. In other colonies, as would become the law when the United States was founded, religion was separate from government. But in the Massachusetts Bay Colony, in order to become a voting member of the community, one had to agree to practice the Puritan religion in full.

PURITAN CITIES

The Puritans were among the first Europeans to settle in New England in what is now Massachusetts. While the Massachusetts Bay Colony did not last, its members founded the cities of Plymouth, Salem, and Boston, which remain in the state of Massachusetts today.

As the Massachusetts Bay Colony grew, Puritans continued to flee England to brave the New World. Settlers built strong houses to withstand the cold winters. They planted fields

The Puritans came to America to pursue religious freedom, but their government imposed the Puritans' religion on all citizens.

and tended livestock. Furs and other goods from the colony were sent back to England to be sold or traded for supplies and materials. By 1640, nearly 20,000 Puritans were living in the Massachusetts Bay Colony. Soon after, the colony had cut its ties to England and was an independent commonwealth. For more than four decades, the Massachusetts Bay Colony remained a theocratic commonwealth in the New World.

As the colony grew and prospered, people of different religious beliefs arrived. However, in order to maintain Puritanism in the colony, the governor and leaders enforced the very type of persecution that had driven them from England: they imposed their religion upon others in the colony under penalty of exile or death.

The challenges to the Massachusetts Bay Colony's theocracy, and the way their leaders handled challengers, provides insight into theocracies today. In deciding that one religion will be the law of the land, very few theocratic leaders allow for freedom of religion.

What Is a Theocracy?

The word *theocracy* derives from the Greek words *theos*, meaning god, and *kratos*, meaning power. A theocracy is a form of government in which power is centered in the divine as understood by a particular religion. In a theocracy, religious laws shape and rule the society. Theocracy is unique among governing systems because no other political systems are based on religious beliefs or the power of the divine.

When discussing theocracies, it is important to distinguish between religion and theocracy. All theocracies are based on religion, but religion does not necessarily influence all governments. For example, a Puritan living in the Massachusetts Bay Colony would likely have practiced the same religion in another colony, such as Virginia. The difference is that in the Massachusetts Bay Colony, Puritanism was the required religion to become a voting member of the community, and it informed governance and legislature.

Theocracies have existed since the beginning of civilization and in all parts of the world. They have governed commonwealths, such as the Massachusetts Bay Colony; empires, such as ancient Egypt; territories, including the Utah Territory in early America; and nations, such as the Islamic Republic of Iran. Theocratic governments have been based on almost every major religion in the world, including Christianity, Islam, Judaism, and various polytheistic religions.

In the Massachusetts Bay Colony, the religion of the colony and governance was Puritanism, a form of Christianity based on the teachings of John Calvin. This form of Christianity was referred

JOHN CALVIN

John Calvin was born in France in 1509. His father, an attorney, wanted his son to follow in his footsteps, and initially, Calvin attended the university to study law. But his interest in religious studies soon triumphed. Calvin lived during a time of great changes in the church and was one of its primary reformers. The religion he founded, Calvinism, emphasized independent churches in which ministers were equal to one another, which was very different from the hierarchical church structure of the time. Calvin also emphasized each individual's personal relationship with God and stressed morality and hard work as the key to salvation. He was influential to the Puritans' theocracy in the Massachusetts Bay Colony and developed a theocratic society in Geneva, Switzerland, where he lived later in his life.

to as Calvinism. Its principles included the divine sovereignty of God and predestination. The Puritans in America believed in hard work and choice, if not of religion, of the people of each church community to elect their leaders. They believed a relationship with God was established through reading the Bible; therefore, they taught their children to read and write, so they could receive religious education from a young age.

Although there are exceptions, most theocratic leaders throughout history have made choices that mirror those of the leaders of the Massachusetts Bay Colony. They maintain strict adherence to the religion by all and promote religious education.

Questioning Theocracy

As the Massachusetts Bay Colony grew, not all of the new settlers wanted to practice the Puritans' religion as strictly as the colony's leaders demanded. One of these challengers was a young clergyperson named Roger Williams. He had originally left England because his radical religious ideas were rejected there. He believed in the freedom to practice whatever form of religion one chose. He preached tolerance and freedom of choice. Although he was expelled from the Massachusetts Bay Colony because he would not practice the Puritans' religion and because of his revolutionary religious beliefs, his ideas proved ahead of their time and eventually became the basis of the US Constitution.

The Quakers were a religious group who came to the Massachusetts Bay Colony in 1656. Their religious beliefs also differed from those of the Puritans. The Puritans' governing body signed a law that exiled the Quakers, stating they would be killed if they returned. Though many left, four Quakers returned to challenge the law and were eventually hanged.

Women proved another challenge to the Puritan leaders' beliefs and rules. Even though she, too, was a Puritan, Anne Hutchinson challenged the fact that only men could become ministers and voters and participate in meetings to discuss the colony's law and religion. In protest, Hutchinson held meetings in her home, inviting women to discuss theology and governance. The men in charge ordered Hutchinson to stop and finally expelled her from the colony. Just as other theocracies share a lack of tolerance for different belief systems, many theocracies restrict women's freedoms and rights as well.

"CITY ON A HILL"

In 1630, the Massachusetts Bay Colony's governor, John Winthrop, gave a sermon urging citizens to create a model community: "For we must consider that we shall be as a city upon a hill, the eyes of all people are upon us."[1] His speech also emphasized the people's special pact with God and their responsibility to build an ideal society in the New World. This speech became known as the "City on a Hill" speech and has inspired several US politicians, including Presidents John F. Kennedy and Ronald Reagan.

Fundamentalism

What theocracy looks like and how a theocratic society is shaped depend not only on the religion but also on the degree of severity of the religion practiced. Those who establish, lead, and maintain theocracies tend to be fundamentalists. Fundamentalism was first defined in the United States during the twentieth century. The characteristics of fundamentalism include literal interpretation of scriptures and religious dogma and a lack of tolerance for other religions or alternate interpretations of codes of conduct or beliefs. Most religions have extreme, radical, or fundamentalist practitioners, but this does not mean that everyone who practices that religion is a fundamentalist. Theocracies based on fundamentalist religion represent an extreme version of the religion and should not be confused with describing any one religion in its entirety.

Religious historian Karen Armstrong has stated, "Fundamentalists feel that they are battling against forces that threaten their most sacred values."[2] This statement can lend insight to the Puritans' intolerance and provide explanation for why fundamentalists govern most theocracies and enforce strict religious practices and beliefs on all citizens. These theocratic rulers believe so much is at risk that their extreme measures are justified.

Church and State

The Massachusetts Bay Colony was a successful and independent theocracy. For nearly 50 years, the colony thrived and prospered under its wealthy and educated founders. It was so successful that the king of England wanted to take control of it, but residents of the Massachusetts Bay Colony gathered a militia, and the king backed down. Shortly before his death in 1685, King Charles II dissolved the colony's charter—for reasons related to money and not religion—and the territory eventually merged with the short-lived Dominion of New England. In 1691, the original Massachusetts Bay Colony became a part of the unified royal colony of Massachusetts. The original religious laws were repealed, and the theocracy ended.

At the end of the American Revolution in 1783, the Treaty of Paris was signed, recognizing the independence of the United States. The founders of the United States of America then addressed the issue of religion and government. Like the Puritans, many of them had come

RELIGIOUS FREEDOM BY LAW

In 1789, James Madison introduced a series of articles to the Constitution, including one for freedom of religion. The wording of the article was debated and discussed, and it eventually became the First Amendment in the Bill of Rights of the Constitution of the United States. It states,

Congress shall make no law respecting an establishment of religion, or prohibiting the free exercise thereof; or abridging the freedom of speech, or of the press; or the right of the people peaceably to assemble, and to petition the government for a redress of grievances.[3]

to North America to practice freedom of religion, and they wanted that freedom built into the new nation's constitution.

In part because of the experiences of challengers to the Massachusetts Bay Colony's theocracy, the founders of the new country introduced a separation between the powers of the church and the powers of the state. Built into the constitution, this separation was meant to forever preclude a theocratic government in the United States—and it has. Fundamentalism—a key factor in most theocracies—has been kept at bay from the country's systems of power. Meanwhile, theocratic governments overseas continue to make a unique impact on international relations, politics, economics, and social conditions around the world. ⌘

RELIGIOUS US CONSTITUTION?

The United States Constitution begins, "We the people of the United States . . ." rather than, "Recognizing Almighty God as the source of all authority and power in civil government . . ."[4] For this, Americans can thank Abraham Lincoln, the sixteenth president of the United States. The second version was given to him by fundamentalist Protestants suggesting that the Constitution be revised to recognize God and Jesus as primary powers in life. Lincoln rejected the revision. Had he worked to include it, and had it been accepted, the United States could have been interpreted as having a theocratic government.

2

Power Dynamics in Theocracies

In a theocracy, religion and government are not separated, as they are in the United States; rather, they are integrally linked. Religious laws overlap with governmental laws. For example, in the Islamic Republic of Iran, the national religion is Islam. Although the Islamic Republic of Iran has a democratic substructure built into the state, it is considered a theocracy because Islamic religious laws dictate the laws and civil codes of conduct.

Theocracies tend to be ruled by one powerful individual. Because any form of religion can become the basis of a theocracy, understanding

Ayatollah Khomeini is pictured on an Iranian banknote.

of the divine varies from one theocracy to another. However, these governments share the concept that their leaders are endowed with, or directly linked to, a divine power. Theocratic rulers either claim to be divine or to have personal contact with the divine.

SIKH THEOCRACY

Jarnail Singh Bhindranwale, also known as Jarnail Singh, was the leader of Damdami Taksal, a religious school in India based on the Sikh religion. Bhindranwale urged a return to the original form of the Sikh religion. He influenced many people in the Punjab region of India around the mid-twentieth century. Bhindranwale supported a theocratic state based on the Sikh religion in the Indian state of Khalistan. He was killed by the Indian Army on charges of separatism, or trying to secede from the country. This led Sikhs to see Bhindranwale as a religious martyr. After his death, many Sikh youth left India for Pakistan.

Examples of Theocratic Rulers

In the Islamic Republic of Iran, the main religious leader is the ayatollah, who is also called the supreme leader. The ayatollah is the chief of state, while the elected president is the head of state under the ayatollah. As of 2010 in Iran, the president claims much more power for himself than ever before, while the ayatollah's power is more restricted than in the past by factions within the state.

Another theocratic community was the ancient Aztec society, which existed in the area that is now Mexico in the fourteenth, fifteenth, and sixteenth centuries. The Aztecs' theocracy was based on a polytheistic religion. When the people's leader offered a drop of sacrificial blood, he was believed to be transformed into a god. According to Aztec historians,

> In the leading city of Tenochtitlán, the city leaders led the empire. . . . The leader was known as the Huey Tlatcani, or Great Speaker. This was the emperor, who was worshipped as a god.[1]

In the early days of the United States, the religious and political leader Joseph Smith proclaimed a personal connection with the divine: an angel had visited him and gave him golden plates that he translated into the Book of Mormon. The Mormon religion provided the basis of a theocratic territory in the area that is now Utah, which Smith ruled until his death in 1844.

Each leader is unique, but most theocratic leaders share certain characteristics. For example, they have almost always been men. They share a capacity for visions of the divine, or some form of direct communication with divine powers, which continues to inform their leadership and governance. Theocratic leaders also tend to share an authoritarian style of leadership.

Who Else Is Included in the Ruling Government?

There is no single template for what a theocracy looks like; each theocratic government is organized differently, with different government positions and branches. Some theocracies, such as the Islamic Republic of Iran, have elected leaders and religious leaders who govern the country. The tradition of democracy is so powerful in Iran that the fundamentalist clerics who took over the country after the 1979 revolution did not try to abolish it. Along with the president, elected officials in Iran include members of the National Assembly, or legislative body, called the Majlis-e-Shuray-e Islami.

People who want to run for most governmental positions in the Islamic Republic of Iran must first be approved by the ayatollah. The 290 elected members of the National Assembly each serve four-year terms. Appointed members of the Iranian government include the 12 members of the Guardian Council, a governing body that screens potential

FLIP-FLOPPING POSITIONS

Theocratic rulers claim a direct line to the divine and justify all laws and societal and political decisions as divine will. But in various theocracies worldwide, stances have changed with circumstances. For example, Afghan religious leaders pushing for theocratic rule long opposed narcotics as against Islamic rule; however, they altered their point of view to support and participate in the lucrative opium trade. In Iran, theocratic leaders have opposed modernization and scientific laws. Yet, they have embraced technological warfare. In the theocratic Mormon territory, leaders preached pristine morality but justified polygamy.

political candidates and has the authority to veto legislation it considers inconsistent with the constitution or Islamic law.

In the Vatican, the government center of the Roman Catholic Church, the primary leader is the pope. Beneath the pope lies a hierarchy of leaders. The pope's advisers are the cardinals, and below them, the bishops. Power is spread among them, but the pope remains the religious and political leader of the sovereign, or independent, country of the Vatican.

THE POPE'S DUAL RULING POWERS

The pope, the Vatican's ruler, oversees two territories. He rules the Vatican, the nation consisting of approximately 800 people, but he also is the supreme ruler of the Holy See, which is the government of the Roman Catholic Church.

In ancient Mayan society, a small group of priests held the highest positions in society. They interpreted life cycles, and if bad things were happening, they made human sacrifices to appease the appetites of the gods and to restore order.

Parliaments, priests, and presidents aid a theocracy's supreme leader, but they are also subject to the divinely empowered leader, who remains in control of the religion, branches of government, and all aspects of civil, social, and cultural life. The people who surround and support the leader practice and enforce the overlapping religious and governmental laws.

How Do Theocratic Leaders Gain and Keep Power?

Theocratic leaders claim to derive power from the divine, but how they achieve governmental control depends on the era of history, locations in the world, and temperament of the leaders. Since the earliest civilizations, theocracies have come to exist in several ways, including through violent takeovers of existing governments and through historical rule of kings and queens.

The Islamic Republic of Iran was established as a modern theocracy in 1979. When people grew discontented with the leader of the nation, Reza Shah Pahlavi, religious leaders gained new adherents and eventually forced the shah, or king, into exile. Under the leadership of the new leader, Ayatollah Ruholla Mussaui Khomeini, the government became an Islamic theocracy.

The laws of theocratic governments are based on religious laws and codes. Leaders maintain control by forcefully imposing religious law on all areas of life. Most theocracies throughout history have had a strong military

AYATOLLAH AND MAN OF THE YEAR

Ayatollah Khomeini was the first ayatollah of the Islamic Republic of Iran. In 1979, *Time* magazine named him Man of the Year stating, "Rarely has so improbable a leader shaken the world."[2] *Time* also recognized him as one of the 100 most influential people of the twentieth century.

Mormon leader Joseph Smith, 1879

Also in the early American colonial years, the leaders of the Massachusetts Bay Colony were chosen through elections. But only those members of the colony who could demonstrate their full religious faith and affiliation were allowed to vote. In this way, democratic elections were blended with religious governance to elect new leaders. ⌘

3

Theocracies in the Ancient World

Theocracies throughout history have varied, depending on the religion that supports the government. There is no single religion that is designated for a theocracy. Followers of Christianity, Islam, Judaism, Buddhism, and other religions have either created or attempted to create theocratic governments. In the ancient world, theocracies were more common than they have been in contemporary times.

Many theocracies in the ancient world were based on polytheistic religions, which center on a belief in many gods or goddesses. Religious

The pharaohs of ancient Egypt were considered divine.

scholars view polytheism as growing out of animism, the belief that everything is alive or animated with a soul. Polytheistic religions include Hinduism, Shintoism, and the ancient Greek religion. Some ancient societies with theocratic governments based on polytheistic belief systems include ancient Egypt and the Aztec Empire.

Ancient Egyptian Theocracy

The ancient Egyptian society thrived in the lower Nile Valley, in the land that is now Egypt, from 3300 BCE to 332 BCE, when Alexander the Great conquered it. In ancient Egypt's theocracy, a pharaoh, who was considered divine, was the head of the religion, the government, and the military.

Beneath the pharaoh were two viziers, who governed the two areas of upper and lower Egypt, and other officials who supported them. Also beneath the pharaoh were the high priests and many priests and priestesses. The position of high priest was handed down through the ruling family on the maternal side, so the son of the pharaoh's oldest daughter inherited the position. Sometimes a woman held the position. Ancient Egypt was one of the few theocracies in which women have held positions of significant power.

Religion was pivotal to all aspects of life in ancient Egypt. Maat, the principle of order or harmony, was considered to be a vital spiritual necessity that the pharaoh had to uphold. In this way, religion contributed to the making of an ordered and just society.

Ancient Egyptian gods were considered to be part human and part divine. They governed all aspects of life. Some of these divinities included Ra, the sun god; Isis, the goddess of magic; and Nut, the sky goddess. One of the most powerful gods was Osiris, the god of the underworld. Ancient Egyptians believed in the possibility of living forever with Osiris in the realm of the gods. They developed elaborate funeral rites, including mummification, so that leaders could live well in the afterlife. Mummies were housed in tombs also believed to be the homes of gods.

Ancient Egyptian society was based on a hierarchy of social classes, but classes were not absolute. The Egyptians developed a written language; literacy was highly valued and accessible to all members of society. Even the poorest members of society could attend writing school and thus be eligible to learn and move up the ranks of society to become members of the priesthood or the government, which often overlapped.

FEMALE PHARAOH

One of few female rulers of ancient Egypt, Queen Hatshepsut was the pharaoh during the eighteenth dynasty, in the fifteenth century BCE. Although she was considered a very beautiful woman, the queen is sometimes portrayed wearing a false beard and the crown of a male ruler. She reigned successfully, building a temple and leading trade expeditions that enriched her land.

In addition to serving in religious roles, priests served as lawyers, healers, and teachers.

Theocracies in Mesoamerica

From about 5000 BCE until the sixteenth century CE, numerous advanced societies flourished in Mesoamerica, the area of the world that is now Mexico and Central America, including the Mayan, Aztec, Olmec, Toltec, and Inca civilizations. Though these cultures varied, they interacted with other cultures in the region, influencing each other and developing several similarities. Most had polytheistic spiritual beliefs, and many ancient Mesoamerican societies were theocracies. As with the cultures, theocracies in this area of the world were distinct but shared similar traits.

Two of the most influential theocracies in Mesoamerica were those of the Mayan and the Aztec civilizations. They began in approximately 5000 BCE and continued through the sixteenth century CE.

The Maya

The Mayan civilization was one of the earliest in Mesoamerica. The Mayan civilization, at its height from approximately 200 to 1000 CE, existed in the area that is now southern Mexico and northern Central America, including what is now El Salvador, Guatemala, Belize, and Honduras. Mayan people believed in multiple gods that governed different areas of life, but

The Maya built elaborate stone temples.

primarily agriculture. Their society was made up of numerous small cities.

Mayan rulers included priests and priest-esses at the highest level of society. These rulers governed both religion and politics. It was the responsibility of the rulers to keep the gods happy so society could run smoothly. Mayan religious rituals included sacrificing humans to appease the gods. Mayan rulers also practiced a process called bloodletting, in which they cut themselves to offer their blood as a gift to the gods.

The Aztec

The Aztec civilization existed in the area that is now central Mexico, thriving from 1325 to 1521 CE. An emperor ruled the theocratic government. The emperor was also considered to be a god, and it was forbidden to look directly at the emperor's face. The Aztec religion, like the Mayan religion before it, was based on the belief in and worship of numerous gods and goddesses. As in the Mayan civilization, human sacrifice was used to appease the gods.

MONTEZUMA, AZTEC RULER

Montezuma was the last theocratic ruler of the ancient Aztecs. When the Spanish came, he sent gold and silver to the newcomers, thus revealing the riches of the Aztec nation. The Aztec people determined that their king had betrayed his divine rule. They killed Montezuma, but the Spanish attack was already underway, and they soon conquered the Aztec civilization.

The Aztecs had a strong military and maintained a hierarchal society—one much stricter than that of ancient Egypt. The emperor, the nobility, and the military generals made up the highest ranks of society, followed by merchants, then farmers, and finally slaves. The emperor ruled all aspects of society, from commerce to military. Aztec warriors fought with neighboring people, capturing enemies for human sacrifice and imposing taxes on nearby kingdoms.

Aztec religious beliefs included the legend of Quetzalcóatl, who was a god predicted to visit the Aztec people in human form. When the Spanish invaders came to Mesoamerica, their leader, Hernán Cortés, was mistaken for Quetzalcóatl. Using this unexpected advantage, Spanish forces were able to mount surprise attacks on the Aztec forces. A great many Aztec people were killed by this violence. Many more died from the unfamiliar diseases the Spanish brought, to which the Aztecs had no immunity. The weakened Aztec theocracy ended when Cortés's troops toppled Tenochtitlán, the Aztec's capital.

The Sassanids

Monotheism, the belief in one god, developed after polytheism. Monotheistic religions include Christianity, Judaism, and Islam. While all monotheistic religions are based on the belief in one god, each differs in how to conceive of

MONGOLS AND THEOCRATIC PERSIA

During the thirteenth through fifteenth centuries, the Mongol warriors, initially led by Genghis Kahn, conquered and amassed huge territories from China to Persia. The Mongols were a nomadic people with a shamanistic religion, but they quickly adapted to the advanced societies they conquered in military campaigns. To govern the new lands, they placed themselves in seats of power while allowing local governing bodies to remain in place. In Islamic Persia, the Mongols adopted Persian culture and Muslim traditions, continuing Islamic society under their rule.

and worship that god. The first monotheistic religion is considered to be Zoroastrianism. This religion is based on the prophet Zarathustra, who advocated a belief in one god. But as Zoroastrianism spread, some versions integrated polytheistic religious beliefs.

The Zoroastrian religion played a prominent role in governing the kingdom of the Sassanids in ancient Persia between 226 and 651. The Sassanian Empire was ruled by a monarch and included a vast territory that now encompasses Iran, Iraq, Afghanistan, and parts of Pakistan and Saudi Arabia. In later years, the Sassanian Empire expanded to include present-day Egypt, Jordan, and Lebanon.

Under Sassanian rule, Zoroastrianism informed government, but the emperor was not seen as an emissary of God or endowed with divine qualities, so the government was not strictly a theocracy. In the seventh century, Alexander the Great destroyed much of the Sassanian Empire. The political leaders remained, but Arabic forces, converts to the new religion of Islam, took over the weakened empire in 632. When the Sassanids lost a pivotal battle to the Arabic fighters, Arabic forces overtook Persia and transformed it into essentially the first large Islamic theocracy.

The Golden Age of Islam

The religion of Islam began in the seventh century and spread rapidly throughout Arabia and other parts of the Middle East. Its prophet and founder, Muhammad, preached the belief in one god, or Allah in Arabic, and promoted brotherhood and equality among Muslims. When Islamic warriors claimed victory over Sassanian forces, they gained a large territory with a rich cultural history. The Persian lands, literature, and philosophy contributed greatly to the formerly nomadic Arabic culture, and Persians took leading roles in the new empire. But Muhammad died

IS TIBET A THEOCRACY?

Tibet lies in Asia along China's western border. Religion, specifically Tibetan Buddhism, is integral to the culture. But whether Tibet has ever been a theocracy depends on how an event from the sixteenth century is interpreted.

In 1578, Tibet was given to the Dalai Lamas, the line of spiritual leaders in Tibetan Buddhism. For centuries, China had little involvement with Tibet, and the Dalai Lamas ruled the religion and society. Tibetan leaders believe that the Chinese emperor ceded control of Tibet to the Dalai Lamas, but Chinese authorities insist that the emperor only allowed the Dalai Lamas to control Tibet as a province of China. That the Dalai Lamas serve as spiritual leaders of Tibetan Buddhism is undisputed. But that they have ruled Tibet as a theocracy is in question. From the point of view of many Tibetans, the Dalai Lama is the religious and political leader of the territory. But from the perspective of the Chinese government, Tibet has remained under Chinese rule.

The Dalai Lamas maintained spiritual and, officially or not depending on one's perspective, political leadership of Tibet. But in the eighteenth century, China took control of Tibet. And in 1950, the nation invaded Tibet, claiming it as part of the People's Republic of China. Leadership of the region remains disputed as of 2010.

The Dome of the Rock in Jerusalem, completed in 691 CE, is the oldest Islamic building in the world.

the same year Arabic forces overtook Persia, and he did not leave a successor.

Muhammad's followers chose a close adviser, Abu Bakr, as the first caliph, or successor of Muhammad. The caliph is recognized as the head of the community of Islam. As spiritual and political leader of Persia, the caliph led a period that came to be known as the Golden Age of Islam. This Islamic theocracy was characterized by religious tolerance and expansive cultural and scientific advancements.

The Golden Age of Islam ended in 999 with the invasion of Turkish forces under Mahmud of Ghazni, whose aggressive military campaigns expanded Muslim territory to include much of what is now India. Persia was invaded again in 1218 by the armies of Genghis Khan, whose secular forces took to the Persian culture and adopted the religion of Islam. The thirteenth through fifteenth centuries witnessed the rise of a more fundamentalist form of Islam in Persia. The next Islamic dynasty began in 1501, when the Safavid Empire took control of Persia under a secular monarchy but established Islam as the state religion. ⌘

4

The Islamic Republic of Iran

The land that was once called Persia has a long history with Islam. It has not always been a theocracy, but the history of the Islamic Republic of Iran is tied to the history of Islam.

In approximately 570 CE, the prophet Muhammad, the founder of Islam, was born in the Arabian Desert. He preached that there was one supreme god, Allah. The local nomads practiced polytheism and initially rejected Muhammad's teachings. Muhammad traveled to Medina, Saudi Arabia, where Islam took root and spread rapidly to Persia and beyond.

In 2005, Ayatollah Khamenei, far left, led Iranians in prayer at the end of Ramadan, the Muslim holy month.

He returned to his homeland, destroyed the polytheistic temple, and made it a holy place for Islam—Mecca. Islam was radical for its belief in one god and its profession of equality for all. The word Islam means submission to the will of God. Muhammad's Islam stressed equality and justice.

Split of Islam

When Muhammad died, he did not leave a successor, and the line of leadership over what was by then a vast empire was unclear. A division soon occurred in Islam. Muhammad's followers chose a close adviser, Abu Bakr, as the first caliph, or successor of Muhammad. The followers of Abu Bakr became known as Sunni Muslims. But Muhammad's daughter, Fatima, was married to a man named Ali, and many saw Ali as the rightful leader. Ali's followers were called Shia Ali—today, Shia Muslims. Explained Gregory Gause, professor of Middle East politics at the University of Vermont,

> Shia believed that leadership should stay within the family of the Prophet. And thus they were the partisans of Ali, his cousin and son-in-law. Sunnis believed that leadership should fall to the person who was deemed by the elite of the community to be best able to lead the community. And it was fundamentally that political division that began the Sunni-Shia split.[1]

During the seventh century, Ali gained power in the area that is now Iraq and was chosen as the fourth caliph. But he died in battle, and his youngest son, Hussein, was killed fighting for his father's position.

Shia call their leaders imams and attribute more powers to them than Sunnis attribute to their Muslim clerics. Ali and Hussein were both imams, or leaders, of Shiite Islam. Professor Gause stated,

> Some of the Sunnis believe that some of the Shia are actually attributing almost divine qualities to the imams, and this is a great sin, because it is associating human beings with the divinity. And if there is one thing that's central to Islamic teaching, it is the oneness of God.[2]

A great number of Shiites also believe in the coming of a hidden twelfth imam, another significant difference between Sunni and Shiite Muslims. Shia make up a minority of Muslims worldwide, approximately ten percent, but they predominate in the oil-rich lands of Iraq, Saudi Arabia, and the theocratic Islamic Republic of Iran. Although Sunni Islam ruled Persia for centuries, in 1500, the Safavid dynasty took control of the land that is now Iran and established it as a Shia stronghold, which it remains to this day.

The Struggle between Tradition and Reform

The Safavids ruled Persia from 1502 to 1736. From the late eighteenth century through 1925, the territory was a religious monarchy, much like Saudi Arabia today, ruled by a shah, or supreme ruler. The Quajar family enforced a strict interpretation of Islam, and women were not allowed to participate in most areas of society. But the people resented the ruling family's lavish lifestyle, and, in 1921, the dynasty was successfully overthrown by a military coup under the leadership of Reza Khan, a former military officer.

Reza Khan adopted the last name Pahlavi, after Iran's original language, and was named shah in 1925. Reza Shah Pahlavi began a campaign to modernize the nation, including establishing a cross-country railway and public school system, developing the nation's industry, and reforming the judiciary. In 1935, Pahlavi changed the country's name from Persia to Iran and asked the international community to adopt the new name. Mohammad Reza Pahlavi, known as the shah—or leader—of Iran, replaced his father as ruling monarch in 1941 and pledged to continue his father's reforms.

In 1951, the shah appointed Mohammad Mosaddeq premier of the country due to the popularity of nationalizing the Iranian oil industry, a movement that Mosaddeq led. But the shah and Mosaddeq disagreed over the oil issue, and in 1953, the shah tried to remove the premier. However, Mosaddeq and his supporters revolted and drove the shah out of the country. With the help of the US Central Intelligence Agency (CIA), the shah and his supporters ousted Mosaddeq. This began a period of authoritarianism that lasted until the revolution in the late 1970s.

A Turkish postage stamp from 1978 displays the image of Reza Shah Pahlavi.

In 1963, the shah launched what is known as the White Revolution, a set of reforms that included improvements in education and voting rights for women. Religious leaders rebelled at what they perceived as affronts against Islamic law and built up a resistance to the shah's rule. Although he spread modernization, his land reforms were very badly carried out and ended up displacing thousands of Iranians from the rural areas to the cities. The people flooded into the urban centers without jobs or prospects, overburdening the state and gathering together to voice their discontent. This, together with the shah's dictatorial rule and denial of democratic reforms, angered the public.

The Islamic cleric Ayatollah Khomeini, who had been exiled by the shah more than a decade earlier for spreading radical religion, returned to the country and capitalized on the discontent to spread fundamentalism and foment revolt. In 1979, after 38 years on the throne, the shah was forced into exile with his family. He went first to Egypt and eventually to the United States, where he was admitted to a hospital for cancer. Muslim leaders in Iran were angered at the United States' support of the shah, and religious fundamental-ists protested in front of the US Embassy in Tehran, seizing 66 US citizens hostage. Fifty-two hostages were held for 444 days in what became known as the Iran hostage crisis.

A Modern Theocracy

At the end of March 1979, the nation voted on a national referendum to establish the Islamic Republic of Iran. The next day, April 1, 1979, was deemed the "first day of God's govern-ment" by Ayatollah Khomeini, who was named the imam and supreme ruler of the new the nation.[3] Despite promises of equality prior to his rule, Ayatollah Khomeini quickly concentrated power and established strict codes of conduct for individuals and society. In the new Islamic theocracy, Ayatollah Khomeini eliminated the many social and cultural reforms instituted by the Pahlavi shahs over the previous five decades.

Ayatollah Khomeini ruled until his death in 1989. During that time, he instituted what is known as the Cultural Revolution, a widespread movement to base the social and cultural life of the nation on his strict inter-pretation of Islamic law. Citizens who protested the reforms were jailed or sentenced to death. Books that Islamic leaders deemed inap-propriate were burned. Women attended segregated schools and workplaces. Dancing and alcohol were forbidden. Although a president was elected and served, Ayatollah Khomeini remained the supreme leader and retained authority over elections, including deciding who could run. In June 1989, Ayatollah Khomeini fell

AMERICANS HELD HOSTAGE IN IRAN

On November 4, 1979, angry religious fundamentalist protestors stormed the US embassy in Iran. They attacked embassy workers and took American prisoners. They held 52 hostages for 444 days. Despite efforts on behalf of President Jimmy Carter, the hostages were not released until the day after the new president, Ronald Reagan, was inaugurated. After the hostages were released, alle-gations surfaced that Reagan's campaign director had secretly met Iranian authorities to arrange for the release of the hostages after Reagan's election. The allegations were not formally substantiated, but the hostage crisis, and its surprising resolution, shook the nation.

ill and died in a hospital. His successor, Ayatollah Ali Khamenei, had served as president and was committed to the same extremist religious ideals as his predecessor.

Today, life in the Islamic Republic of Iran remains dramatically different from the way it was under the Pahlavi shahs. Then, women could dress as they pleased and hold professional positions; as of 2010 women must wear chadors and be accompanied by male escorts in public. Women are not allowed to look directly at men or to call attention to themselves in any way, and they must remain in segregated women-only areas in public. Since the Cultural Revolution, intellectuals and liberals, including many academics, authors, journalists, and artists, have been forced to hold their ideas in check or risk imprisonment or death. Government-run schools in the Islamic Republic of Iran teach the fundamentalist aspects of Islam. Moral police

FATWA FOR MUSLIM WRITER

In 1989, Salman Rushdie, the Indian writer who was raised Muslim and was living in England, published his fourth novel, *The Satanic Verses.* The work of fiction is partly based on the life of Muhammad and includes references to the Koran. In February 1989, Ayatollah Khomeini issued a fatwa, or religious ruling, ordering Muslims to kill Rushdie for what he considered to be a book that is blasphemous to Islam.

force citizens to follow strict codes of behavior. Punishments for being too Western, for suspected adultery, or for dissension are harsh and include death by hanging and stoning.

Elections are held in the Islamic Republic of Iran, but the Iranian people have demonstrated discontent with what they perceive as unfair electoral processes. Late in the twentieth century and early in the twenty-first, Iranians mounted large-scale protests in favor of fairer elections and against the nation's authoritarian theocratic rule. The government responded with strict curfews and sporadic violence, jailing leaders of the dissent and enforcing an end to the street protests. ⌘

PEACE PRIZE FOR MUSLIM LAWYER

In 2003, lawyer and activist Shirin Ebadi became the first Muslim and Iranian woman to win the Nobel Peace Prize. In 1975, she was the first female judge in Iran. In 1979, she was forced to resign because women were not considered fit to be judges. She opened a law practice and handled many political criminal cases and supported human rights. In 2009, Ebadi was exiled from Iran for protesting the 2009 Iranian presidential election.

5

The Vatican

The Vatican is the world's longest-running theocracy. Today, it occupies approximately .17 square miles (.44 sq km) in Vatican City, located within Rome, and is the smallest independent nation in the world. In earlier centuries, the Vatican occupied vast territories in Italy and parts of France, and its influence on government, politics, economics, and civic life was extensive. Today, the Vatican continues to rule the religious life of Catholics worldwide, but its political and geographic territory remains concentrated in a small section of the city of Rome.

Vatican City hosts world-renowned architecture, including Saint Peter's Basilica and Sant'Angelo's Bridge.

Pope Pius IX, 1872

This consisted of three agreements between the governments of Italy and the Vatican. The first recognized the sovereignty of the Vatican and established the territorial boundaries of Vatican City. The second made Catholicism the state religion of Italy (an agreement superseded in 1984, when Italy was made a secular state). The third agreement was economic; it addressed financial claims the Vatican made on Italy for annexing the Papal States a century earlier. The treaty granted funds to the Vatican, with interest, dissolving any claims the Vatican had for funds owed by the Italian government.

As of 2010, the Vatican is a sovereign state with independent foreign relations and political and religious control over Vatican City. Approximately 800 people, including the pope, live in Vatican City in Rome. Inside, the pope, supported by the cardinals, has full political and religious control. Outside, the pope is the sovereign head of state. As such, he can make agreements and treaties with other heads of state, be represented at the UN, and sign international agreements and treaties. Although, technically, the Vatican could wage war, it lacks an air force or navy and maintains a strong stance in support of human life and against warfare.

Life in the Vatican

A wall surrounds the Vatican, dividing it from the city of Rome. In addition to the Papal residence, the Vatican houses basilicas and chapels, including the famous Sistine Chapel. The Basilica of Saint Paul, also part of the Vatican, lies outside the wall in the city of Rome. The Vatican also manages a world-class museum, an extensive library and archives, a publishing house, and a radio station. Throughout its long history, the Vatican has sponsored numerous schools worldwide and has played an important role in the history of art and architecture, commissioning many important works, several of which remain in the Vatican today.

Writing for the *National Catholic Reporter,* Michael K. Holleran described a video, *Daily Life in the Vatican,* by Films for the Humanities and Sciences. Holleran stated,

> Though it strives to inject a lighter tone by showing sisters [nuns] at evening recreation, playing cards and watching soccer, the video creates a rather intense and stringent atmosphere by its emphasis on the Vatican as a city-state, with all its protocol and unassailable decorum.[2]

This picture of the Vatican as a sovereign organization, rife with ceremony, captures the essence of this small, but powerful, theocracy.

Hierarchy in the Vatican

In the early days of Christianity, the church decided that ordained priests could not marry. It also established the doctrine of the Holy Trinity, which proclaimed three parts to the divine: God the Holy Father, the Holy Son, and the Holy Ghost. Each of these iterations of God is male, and the leaders

GRAND ARCHITECTURE

Many of the Vatican's oldest buildings are its churches. The Basilica of Saint John Lateran, built by Roman Emperor Constantine, was the first church in Rome. It is dedicated to Saint John the Baptist, the historical figure who baptized Jesus, and is the official cathedral of the pope. For this distinction, it is known as Omnium urbis et orbis Ecclesiarum Mater et Caput, or Cathedral of Rome and of the World.

of the Catholic Church, too, are all male. Women can take religious vows to become nuns, but nuns do not have the same authority as priests.

The pope is ex officio of the Vatican. In other words, he is the head of government of Vatican City and the supreme pontiff, or leader, of the Catholic Church. He is deemed infallible in moral and ethical matters; his followers believe him to be the ultimate authority in moral and ethical questions. His position is at the head of a hierarchy of clergy.

The leaders of the government of Vatican City are appointed by the pope, who can dismiss them at any time. They include the secretary of state, the president of the Pontifical Commission for the Vatican City State, and the governor of Vatican City. The cardinals advise the pope and elect a new pope upon his death. Bishops are teachers, leaders, and ministers of the Vatican at the top level of the clergy. Those responsible for large metropolitan areas are called archbishops. Priests give sacraments,

"What man needs most cannot be guaranteed to him by law. In order to live life to the fullest, something more intimate is necessary that can be granted only as a gift: we could say that man lives by that love which only God can communicate since He created the human person in His image and likeness."[3]

—*Pope Benedict XVI,
Easter 2010*

As of 2010, Pope Benedict XVI was the head of the Vatican government.

minister church teachings, and oversee churches. Deacons are priests in training.

The Vatican has conservative opinions about women and severely limits their powers of authority. Women cannot become priests on any level. This religious perspective lies in direct opposition to equal rights granted in the

Universal Declaration of Human Rights. Women can take religious vows to become nuns. Due to cultural changes inspired by the women's movement in the United States during the 1970s, US nuns have been the subjects of Vatican scrutiny. In 2001, the Vatican expressed concerns about the leadership role of US nuns. In 2009, it announced it would lead an examination of the Leadership Conference of Women Religious (LCWR), the largest women's religious organization in the United States, led by Catholic nuns.

The male-only Catholic priesthood is almost as old as the church, and the Vatican continually reaffirms it. In 1994, in a document titled *On the Ordination to the Priesthood*, the Vatican confirmed that the Vatican "has no authority whatsoever to confer priestly ordination on women."[4] The Vatican believes that women are not allowed to be ordained as priests.

The Vatican and International Relations

In centuries past, when it held a larger geographic area, the Vatican was marked by war. During the eleventh through thirteenth centuries, the Vatican was involved in the Crusades, Christian raids against Muslims. In the fifteenth through nineteenth centuries, particularly in Spain, the Vatican sanctioned torture and violence against those it deemed to have incomplete or inadequate faith during what is known as the Inquisition.

As of 2010, the Vatican has the smallest standing army in the world, the Swiss Guard. Membership is restricted to Swiss or Catholic men. Because it has no air force or navy, the Vatican depends on the Italian military for outside protection.

In recent years, the Vatican has undergone extensive international pressure in relation to lawsuits against Catholic priests accused of pedophilia. Citizens of the United States, Canada, Ireland, and other countries have brought forward cases of sexual abuse by priests, casting a shadow over the Vatican's stance in the international community.

ADDRESS TO VICTIMS

In 2007, Cardinal Roger M. Mahony of Los Angeles addressed the largest settlement the Vatican has paid to victims of sexual abuse by priests:

> *It is the shared hope of everyone in our local church that these victims, many of whom suffered in silence for decades, may find a measure of healing and some sense of closure with today's announcement.*[5]

The Vatican supports education and works of charity, including welfare for the poor, around the world. According to the US CIA, as of 2010, the Vatican is not engaged in any international disputes. ⌘

6

Civic Life in a Theocracy

In a theocracy, the government makes and enforces laws based on the state religion. It also passes new laws that derive from religious law. Maulana Maududi, a Pakistani religious and political leader in the twentieth century, expressed this idea clearly in his discussion of an Islamic theocratic state:

> Unlike a Secular state, its duty is not merely to maintain internal order, to defend the frontiers and to work for the material prosperity of the country. Rather its first and foremost obligation is to establish the system of Salat [prayer] and

Women in theocracies are often required to cover their heads and faces in public.

Zakat [alms tax], to [propagate] and establish those things which have been declared to be "virtues" by God and His Messenger, and to eradicate those things which have been declared "vices" by them.[1]

TOLERANT AND EQUAL RELIGIONS

The founders of major world religions, including Jesus of Christianity and Muhammad of Islam, demonstrated tolerance for others' differences and promoted equality for women. The religions that were founded on their beliefs have moved in more restrictive and dogmatic directions. But many devout religious people throughout the world believe in and practice the humane and tolerant versions of these religions as their founders promoted.

No distinction exists between religious law and state law, and often social behavior, in a theocracy. Religion dictates legal codes that govern individual and societal behavior including styles of dress, choice in marriage, and how, when, and where individuals appear in public.

The impact of theocracy on individual freedom does not depend as much on the religion as it does on the interpretation of that religion by political and religious leaders and how these leaders maintain power. Theocracies that interpret religion in a fundamentalist way, and religious law in a strict manner, pose a threat to secular civil rights—including the freedom of religion, speech, and the press. In theocracies that uphold laws using militaristic force, individuals have little choice but to obey. Individuals in such theocratic societies must remain obedient to state-mandated religious laws that govern daily life, politics, economy, education, health care, and all aspects of the culture.

Theocratic governments tolerant of personal choice and individual freedoms have existed. These governments allowed, to varying degrees, freedom of belief and the ability to dress and live as one chooses. Ancient Egypt provides an example of a theocracy with a polytheistic religion that provided for human rights, including equality and advancement, while promoting art and culture in the name of religion. The Golden Age of Islam provides an example of a tolerant and progressive form of theocracy under the monotheistic religion of Islam. At that time, although laws were Islamic, people of different faiths could practice their religions without discrimination.

However, in many theocracies throughout history, leaders have interpreted religious scriptures and laws in a strict way that tends to limit individual choice and freedom. One example of such a theocracy is the Vatican during the Inquisition, when church leaders (synonymous with governmental leaders of the Vatican's Papal States) tortured and killed those whose faith they deemed false or insufficient. In the fifteenth century, the Shia Muslim rule of Persia represented a restrictive theocracy that limited basic human rights, including freedom of religion and dress.

Theocratic versus Secular Societies: The Case of Yemen

In numerous countries today, theocracy is not the official government, but theocratic rulers have taken over and govern parts of the country. One of these countries, Yemen, provides a distinctive look at how civil rights in a theocracy often differ from civil rights in a secular society.

SHARIA

Sharia, or "the way," is Islamic law. It provides a legal framework to govern nearly every area of Islamic life and society, from business and government to sexuality and marriage. Sharia greatly informs the law in the theocratic Islamic Republic of Iran and in Saudi Arabia, Kuwait, Bahrain, Yemen, and the United Arab Emirates and partly influences the law in Pakistan, Egypt, and Iraq, and parts of Nigeria, Algeria, Sudan, Yemen, and Indonesia.

Yemen is a small country in the Middle East. From 1967 to 1986, a Marxist regime governed South Yemen, while North Yemen was a theocratic Islamic state. During that time, men and women were equal citizens in South Yemen. Both were eligible for jobs in the Ministry of Labor, based on their qualifications, and there was no official dress code for men or women. Every citizen received health care and education through college via the Marxist government. At the same time, in North Yemen, Islamic religious law dictated civil law. Men and women did not enjoy the same freedoms because the government interpreted the Koran literally and thus gave women fewer rights than men. Men could marry up to four wives and seek divorce, while women were legally bound to obey their husbands and unable to seek divorce for any reason.

Women and Theocracy

The treatment of women in North Yemen is not atypical in theocracies. Legislation informed by religious law binds all citizens in a theocracy, but women in particular have been subject to strict codes of behavior. How women are treated is

NAIPAUL AND ISLAMIC CULTURE

Author V. S. Naipaul won the Nobel Prize in Literature in 2001. Born in Trinidad to Indian parents, Naipaul has traveled and lived in many places around the world. Two of his books, *Among the Believers* and *Beyond Belief*, are based on his travels around the Muslim world, primarily to Indonesia, Iran, Pakistan, and Malaysia, and his interactions with the Muslim people living in those places. He made his first visit to Iran, Pakistan, and Indonesia during the 1970s, a time of rising fundamentalism, and his second in the 1990s, during a time of growing Islamic conversion. Through stories of the people he met, Naipaul explored how Islam has often taken hold of the minds and hearts of people threatened by modernization and equal rights for women.

one of the most obvious differences between theocratic and secular governments. This is mainly because fundamentalist religious inter- pretations—upon which the majority of historic and contemporary theocracies are based—usually impose strict behavior on women.

Strict religious laws governing women's behaviors are not limited to any one religion and thus are not limited to any specific form of theoc- racy. For example, a conservative interpretation of Halacha, or Jewish religious law, mandates that women remain fully covered and limits the ability of women to hold jobs or positions of power.

Although Sharia is interpreted differently among different Muslim groups, it is the strict interpretation of Sharia that informs the law in the Islamic Republic of Iran and in theocratically governed parts of countries including Sudan, Yemen, Afghanistan, and Pakistan. In these cases, many Western societies believe the law severely limits women's rights by requiring a full covering of the head and body—called a chador in Iran, an abaya in Saudi Arabia, and a burka in Afghani- stan. It also requires the segregation of women and men in public places, and it forbids women to hold positions of power.

Islamic theocracies mete out harsh, even brutal, punishments to women. In the Islamic Republic of Iran, death by stoning is condoned by the government as a punishment for adultery, and women have little recourse to defend them- selves. The Pakistani newspaper *Dawn* published an article on the status of women, particularly in poor and rural areas. It stated,

> The nation remains without a domestic violence law. It has been drafted, but lawmakers say it is still under debate as a senator from a hard-line Islamic party raised objections and sent the bill back to parliament.[2]

Citizens around the world have protested the treatment of women under Islamic theocracies and Sharia. These include many Muslim women who have risked their lives to fight for women's rights in Islamic society, challenging the strict interpretation of religious law that mistreats so

TAKING OFF THE HIJAB

Fariba Davoodi Mohajer is an Iranian journalist and devout Muslim. For many years, she wore the hijab, or head scarf, without question. But as she began to learn more about the treatment of women and girls in her country, she spoke out for greater equality and improved treatment of women. In 2006, while in Ireland, Mohajer removed her veil and threw it in the ocean. "For a moment, I felt that there was no greater pleasure in the world than the feeling of the wind in my hair," she said of that day. Today, she is a human rights activist living in the United States. "I saw the hijab as one of the tools that is being used against women to control them and as a tool for repression," she said. "That's how I see it, and that is why I decided not to wear it any more."[3]

Women in Iran protested gender discrimination during an Iranian Women Movement in 2005.

many women. Women fighting for change in Islamic regimes remain devoted to their religion but promote an interpretation of Islam that treats girls and women with respect, equality, and nonviolence. Asieh Amini, an Iranian poet, journalist and activist, cofounded Zanan-e Iran, a Web site dedicated to the Iranian women's movement. Her actions and other women's protests against the death penalty and stoning for female adulterers have helped to save young women and girls from brutality and execution.

Family Life and Marriage in a Theocracy

In theocracies, whether officially sanctioned theocratic governments or functionally theocratic states, religious laws often dictate how marriage and family life function within a society. Even in countries with secular governments, religious law often prevails in determining laws for marriage and family. For example, in Israel, a democratic country, strict religious law governs deaths, marriages, and adoptions. Secular or non-Orthodox Jewish Israelis may not marry Jewish Israelis within the country. These couples often go to Cyprus or Italy to marry.

Arranged marriages are unions determined by parents, families, or community elders rather than through the choice of the bride and groom. Illegal in the United States, arranged marriages have been advocated, at least at some point, by nearly every world religion and continue to be practiced in many Hindu, Muslim, Orthodox Jewish, and some Christian families. Governments worldwide

RELIGIOUS RULE IN NIGERIA

In Nigeria in 2000, many states in the north formally adopted Sharia as part of the legal system. Even Christians living in northern Nigeria must abide by Islamic law, which includes the banning of alcohol and the segregation of men and women in schools and on public buses.

vary in their legal support of arranged marriage, but it is often sanctioned by religious custom, which takes precedence over governmental law in many rural and poverty-stricken areas of the world.

Some arranged marriages include child brides; the bride (and, less often, the groom) is a child below the legal age for marriage. Child brides are forced into marriage in countries including Egypt, India, Pakistan, and Afghanistan, often in marriages to much older men. UNICEF Child Protection Specialist Sulagna Roy stated, "Child marriage is against child rights. It influences children's and mother's health. It continues a cycle of poverty. It leaves a disempowered girl."[4] Even in non-theocratic countries where it is illegal, the law is often overlooked in rural communities where religious rule predominates.

Religious law also dictates the ending of marriages. Strict interpretations of Islam, Judaism, and Christianity have either denied divorce altogether or, more often, denied it only to women. In parts of Israel where Orthodox Jewish law prevails, women may not seek divorce. In areas of the world governed by fundamentalist Islam, and in parts of India governed by traditional interpretations of Hindu law, women are denied divorce even in cases of severe abuse.

The custom of polygamy has also been sanctioned by religion and in theocratic states. In the Mormon theocracy in the early United states, men were allowed to take multiple wives—founder Joseph Smith is believed to have had 33 wives—whereas women were subject to

Asha, left, was 14 years old when she married her husband, right.

the whims of their husbands. Polygamy is legal in the Islamic Republic of Iran if the man attains permission from his first wife.

The theocracy of the Vatican governs marriage and family life of its citizens. The Vatican's positions on marriage and the family are conservative, denying the legality of de facto unions in which couples live together outside of marriage. The Vatican also forbids abortion, birth control, and divorce.

Dissention and Protest

There is no single way in which theocratic rulers handle dissent. In most examples of theocracy, challengers to the government and religion are treated harshly. Examples of this can be found throughout history, from the Inquisition to contemporary stoning (also a punishment during Biblical times), from the harsh punishments of religious police in Saudi Arabia to the jailing of liberal intellectuals in the Islamic Republic of Iran.

In the Islamic Republic of Iran, men and women are granted the right to vote, but religious leaders ultimately decide the outcome of political elections. The Ayatollah Khomeini maintained approval over anyone running for public office so that no one who threatened strict Islamic law would ever gain power.

This control was called into question in the 2009 presidential election. Millions of Iranians disputed the reported results, claiming voter fraud. The Ayatollah Khamenei settled the question with an investigation, followed by the announcement that President Mahmoud Ahmadinejad had triumphed over his opponent, the more reformist Mir Hossein Mousavi, in his bid for reelection. Again, hundreds of thousands of Iranians took to the streets in protest. Authorities responded by imposing a strict curfew and clamping down on protestors. At least one rally ended in bloodshed, with the Iranian military shooting protestors. During and after the protests, numerous intellectuals and reformists were jailed. ⌘

7

Theocracy, Art, and Education

Around the world and through the centuries, theocratic societies have often been developers and promoters of art and architecture. The depth of theocratic leaders' faith and the extent of their longing to pay tribute to their god or gods has inspired them to commission and construct beautiful works of art and architecture. Theocratic societies have been responsible for many works that have contributed greatly to the histories of both disciplines. Many of these religiously commissioned works were monumental at the time and still are today.

The Sphinx and the Great Pyramid in Egypt

Some of the world's most treasured palaces and structures have been built under theocracies. Ancient Egyptians constructed amazing pyramids in Egypt as elaborate burial places. The elaborate Aztec temples in Mexico were made during the Aztec Empire as places of sacrificial worship. The Vatican has built grandiose cathedrals around the world, including Notre Dame in Paris, France. And Islamic theocracies have constructed beautiful structures, such as the Taj Mahal in Agra, India, for centuries.

The union of religion and government has also been responsible for commissioning great works of art. Theocratic societies have produced paintings, tapestries, carvings, and sculptures to honor the divine. The Vatican has given commissions to some of the most famous artists in history. Raphael made monumental frescoes in the papal palace in the early sixteenth century.

SEVEN WONDERS OF THE ANCIENT WORLD

The Seven Wonders of the Ancient World include monumental structures built during the Classical era. They are the Pyramids of Egypt at Giza, the Hanging Gardens of Babylon, the Temple of Artemis at Ephesus, the statue of Zeus, the Mausoleum at Halicarnassus, the Colossus of Rhodes, and the Lighthouse of Alexandria. All but two of these fantastic structures—the Hanging Gardens of Babylon and the Lighthouse of Alexandria—were commissioned for religious reasons. The Pyramids at Giza in Egypt are the only wonder that still exists.

The Taj Mahal in Agra, India

Michelangelo famously painted the ceiling of the Sistine Chapel, also in the early sixteenth century. The Vatican Museums house a large collection of religious art through the ages.

Specific religious beliefs have led to the development of particular art forms. The ancient Egyptians' belief that kings and queens needed to be preserved, mummified, and buried with riches to accompany them in the afterlife led to the creation of sacred tombs and Egyptian mummies with artistic objects and relics. In Tibet, Buddhism is part of everyday life. Spiritual art, including decorative everyday items, such as furniture and dishes, as well as many kinds of sculpture and intricate paintings on cloth, called *thangkas*, permeates the culture.

Personal Expression, Censorship, and Theocracy

The cultural landmarks constructed during theocracies have supported the state religion. While these works have great artistic merit, they do not result from freedom of expression.

Other forms of creative expression, art and architecture made to express personal ideas or feelings, have rarely benefited from theocratic rule. In theocratic societies, art that challenges the ideals of the theocracy has often been subject to censorship.

One example of censorship by a theocracy is the Vatican's Index Librorum Prohibitorum, or list of censored books. Pope Pius IV issued the first index in 1564. In 1571, the Vatican established the Sacred Congregation of the Index, a group of priests given the authority to determine which books should be on the index. Many of these were religious works that diverged from the teachings of the Vatican, such as books about forms of Christianity other than Catholicism, but works that the congregation deemed immoral were also on the list of banned books. Notable philosophers and writers whose works have appeared on the index include Desiderius Erasmus, Voltaire, Nicolaus Copernicus, Honoré de Balzac, and Jean-Paul Sartre. The index was last updated in 1948. At that time, 4,000 titles were on the list.

Censorship was so common in the early days of the Islamic Republic of Iran that at least two writers have explored the issue in their own works. *Reading Lolita in Tehran*, written by former university professor and Iranian Azar Nafisi and published in 2003, is a memoir about gathering in secret with friends to read books that the government had forbidden. The forbidden books included classics by Vladimir Nabokov, F. Scott Fitzgerald, and Jane Austen. *Censoring an Iranian Love Story*, written by Shahriar Mandanipour and

BUDDHIST STATUES DESTROYED

In March 2001, leaders of the de facto government of the Taliban destroyed two giant statues of the Buddha in central Afghanistan. The statues went against their law of a monotheistic religion and also against the Islamic law prohibiting representation of the human form. Curators, art historians, religious leaders, and others around the world protested and lamented the loss of the ancient statues.

published in 2009, explores life and love in Iran under threat of the religious police. In another example of the kind of censorship carried out by the theocratic government, Mandanipour had been forbidden from publishing fiction from 1992 to 1997. In 1997, elections brought a reformist president, Mohammad Khatami, to power, and the heavy censorship laws were relaxed.

Education in Theocracy

In addition to art and architecture, many theocracies value learning and education. For example, in ancient Egypt, writing was highly valued, and education was a tool for advancement; anyone who held a government position was required to be literate. In Saudi Arabia, which is governed by a monarchy with religious authorities determining cultural codes, the government grants every citizen a free education through the university level.

Education is pivotal to expanding intellect and teaching new ideas, but it can also be used as a tool to indoctrinate students in beliefs and dogma central to a theocratic society. In most theocracies, schools teach religious dogma. Like art, education and literacy can open minds and expand one's possibilities. But too much exploration can threaten the absolutism of a theocracy. If people think in new and different ways, they may challenge the officially accepted theology or the codes of behavior that most theocracies demand. Controlling what schools teach and how people behave is a daily task of religious authorities.

The Vatican and Education

Since the early days of the Roman Catholic Church, when the Vatican controlled parts of Italy and France as well as what is now the Vatican City in Rome, monks have run schools and universities. Today, Vatican-sponsored Catholic schools provide education for children, adolescents, and college students in countries around the world.

The Vatican is an important center for higher education, specifically in training for clergy. In Rome, where Vatican City is located, there are

WOMEN'S EDUCATION IN THE MIDDLE EAST

Although the countries have strict laws concerning women's behavior, Iran and Saudi Arabia have very different educational practices for women from Afghanistan. This is due to religious and political culture, the economic context, and each country's history. Both Iran and Saudi Arabia are very urbanized. For example, after the shah's failed land reforms, hundreds of thousands of Iranians surged into the cities, and approximately half of the population lived in urban areas by the 1970s. Both countries have excellent infrastructures due to their oil wealth. Despite the conservative nature of the religious leadership in Iran and the Saudi king's firm hold on his own power and use of a conservative form of Islam, their urbanized, modern populations have a strong tradition of education for both sexes.

Conversely, Afghanistan is predominantly rural and extremely traditional. It has no important natural resources other than opium. Women have not had nearly as much opportunity to build the educational social norm into their communities, and the rule of the Taliban in the country has set back their efforts by decades, even in the cities.

approximately 65 papal educational institutions for higher learning, including the Pontifical Gregorian University, the Pontifical Biblical Institute, and the Pontifical Institute of Christian Archaeology. The Sacred Congregation for Catholic Education, which is the ministry of the Vatican responsible for education, summarizes the importance of education to the Vatican:

> *In the light of her mission of salvation, the Church considers that the Catholic school provides a privileged environment for the complete formation of her members, and that it also provides a highly important service to mankind.*[1]

Although Vatican-sponsored schools teach a wide range of subjects, church history and dogma are important parts of the curriculum. Vatican-run schools operate in many nations outside Vatican City, sometimes with beliefs and even laws that differ from church code. Since the Second Vatican Council, from 1962 to 1965, the Vatican has focused on the issue of teaching students in cultures around the world, which sometimes means taking into account cultural and religious differences.

Education in the Islamic Republic of Iran

Education is a priority in the Islamic Republic of Iran. The majority of children attend primary school, and many remain in school through the university level. The Ministry of Education and

Training employs more government employees than any other ministry.

Like US students, Iranian students attend preschool, primary school, and middle school. In high school, they can choose an academic or technical path. The academic path prepares students to attend university. The technical path prepares students to enter the work force in the technical, business, or agricultural fields.

Religious education makes up nearly half the curriculum in Iranian schools. Books and curricula that do not support Islamic law or that are deemed immoral are not allowed in Iranian schools. Censorship is prevalent, and many modern classics have been censored from Iranian school and society.

WOMEN'S EDUCATION IN IRAN

While the revolution did substantially restrict women's rights, Iranian women were able to keep the tradition of female education that the shah championed. The number of female students in university has grown in recent years, and they make up approximately 65 percent of university students in Iran.[2] Women are also more visible in public offices and the professional world. Even so, women have to attend separate classrooms and are barred from studying many subjects offered to male students.

Education and Radical Islam

In many poor nations around the world, religious leaders offer children and adolescents the chance to learn and be educated. But often, the price is indoctrination into the school's fundamentalist interpretations of religion. In Afghanistan, a state that is not formally theocratic but continues to struggle with a fragile balance between religious and governmental leaders, tribal clerics of the Taliban, a fundamentalist Islamic faction, have effectively educated many of the nation's youth. Educating students in Afghanistan has greatly increased the numbers of this radical religious group; this indoctrinating type of education has provided the group with new adherents to its radical version of Islam. Only boys and men are allowed to be educated. The Taliban forbids women and girls from attending school, in accordance with the tribal theocratic leaders' strict interpretation of Sharia.

Other fundamentalist Islamic groups have established similar types of schools in several other countries. In 2000, American Jeffrey Goldberg traveled to some of these countries to spend time in the madrasas, or Muslim religious schools, and learn more about them. He visited the Haqqania madrasa in Pakistan, where more than 2,800 students were enrolled. Of his time there, Goldberg noted,

> Haqqania is notable not only because of its size, but also because it has graduated more leaders of the Taliban, Afghanistan's ruling

faction, than any other school in the world, including any school in Afghanistan.[3]

As schools like this one grow and attract more students, radical Islam spreads. This is one social trend that has tipped the balance of power toward theocratic governance in many nations.

Not all Muslim schools are dedicated to securing new followers or teaching fundamentalist religion, however. Many Muslim schools educate students and teach a humane or reformist version of Islam. Still, over the past three decades, fundamentalist madrasas have opened in several countries, including Afghanistan, Malaysia, Indonesia, Yemen, Algeria, Sudan, and Nigeria. The schools provide an education for poor citizens while developing knowledgeable religious leaders in rural areas. ⌘

8

Theocratic Economies

Not all theocratic governments share the same form of economics. What they have in common is that, just as civic life, culture, and the law are informed by religion in theocracies, so are economics. The values of the religion, and the temperament of the ruler or ruling party, contribute to a theocracy's economic standpoint. But the majority of theocratic economics, regardless of the religion, share an interest in equal distribution of resources and value generosity to others.

Oil provides wealth to the Islamic Republic of Iran.

One example of this can be found in the Mormon tradition. Since the early Mormon theocracy, helping those in need has been important to Mormons. This can take the form of money collected from church members to disperse to those in need as well as providing assistance to neighbors. For example, when Hurricane Katrina hit the southern coast of the United States in 2005, Mormons were among the first volunteers to arrive on the scene to provide relief efforts, supporting victims in need of food, clothing, and shelter.

The Islamic Republic of Iran represents a theocracy where equality is built into the economic system. In this country rich with oil, all of the citizens receive free education and health care and none are required to pay taxes. Equality is important to Islam, and, in Iran, all citizens share in the nation's success. Yet, despite the riches, elaborate displays of wealth are uncommon in Iran. They are considered to be outside the strict religious culture, where aspects of capitalism, including displays of wealth and focus on the individual, are rejected in the name of equality, modesty, and community.

Saudi Arabia represents a wealthy Islamic nation where the displays of riches evident in successful free market capitalism are not as widely shunned. The elaborate taste of the Saud royal family is well documented. The ruling family owns stables of expensive Saudi Arabian racehorses and commissions extravagant architecture, including a replica of Spain's Alhambra, a beautiful palace that remains from a time of

Saudi Arabian wealth benefits citizens: they receive free education and do not have to pay taxes.

Moorish rule. But the equality and community so integral to Islam also influence the Saudi Arabian economy; citizens do not pay taxes and are also given free education and health care.

An exception to the common theme of generosity and equality can be found in the fundamentalist Christian communities of the United States; universal government-sponsored health care is usually rejected in favor of free market capitalism. Though these communities do not constitute a theocracy, conservative Christian politicians represent their views in government and their voices are heard in elections.

Islamic Economics

Islamic economics is the most widespread form of theocratic economics. In recent decades, it has spread to countries all over the world, including both Muslim countries and Muslim areas of non-Muslim countries. Of modern Islamic economics, economist Timur Kuran wrote, "Islamic economics applies ancient solutions to perceived problems of the *present*; and where such solutions are lacking, it seeks scriptural justification for its favored reforms."[1] The primary feature that distinguishes Islamic economics from others is that it strives to eliminate interest. But this is only one aspect of a comprehensive economic system that includes trade, banking, and consumer behavior.

Contemporary Islamic economics is relatively new, but it is based on ancient principles, dating back to the earliest days of Islam in seventh century Arabia. Early Islamic writers included economic principles as part of a wider cultural framework. The writings of Sayyid Abul-A'la Maududi in the twentieth century have

STUDYING ISLAMIC ECONOMICS

A number of organizations and periodicals are dedicated to the study of Islamic economics. Two of these include the International Center for Research in Islamic Economics at King Abdulaziz University in Jeddah, Saudi Arabia, and the International Association for Islamic Economics in Leicester, England.

had a large impact on today's Islamic economics as well. This Pakistani social philosopher believed in Islam as a way of life and laid the foundations for many Islamic disciplines, including economics. Other primary contributors to the discipline of Islamic economics include Sayyid Muhammad Baqir al-Sadr of Iraq and Sayyid Qutb of Egypt, who lived in the twentieth century as well. These three thinkers diverge on specifics, but they agree that Islamic economics corrects what they

FUNDAMENTALIST ECONOMICS

Duke University economics professor and author Timur Kuran has defined what he calls fundamentalist economics to describe the policies of fundamentalist forms of religious governments in regard to economics. Kuran wrote,

> Fundamentalist economics is largely a reaction to perceived injustices in existing economic systems and to transformations engendered by the industrial revolution, the expansion of government, and the information revolution.[2]

Fundamentalist economists share the sense that these changes have corrupted culture and necessitate a greater morality that can be achieved through a religiously informed system of economics. In Kuran's estimation, secular economic theories define human wants as limitless, whereas fundamentalist economics seek to instill in humans greater moderation through religious morality. Fundamentalist economic theory, Kuran wrote, "asserts that the collective good requires the individual to subordinate his own interests to those of the wider community."[3]

perceive as inherent immoralities in the capitalist and socialist systems.

Islamic economics are based on an idealistic interpretation of the Golden Age of Islam in the seventh century. One distinguishing feature of Islamic economics, the elimination of interest, derives from this time. Interest is seen as encouraging greed and corruption. The first Islamic bank, which practiced trade and offered loans without the use of interest, opened in Cairo, Egypt, in 1971. Today, Islamic banks exist in countries around the world, including Muslim areas of non-theocratic countries and partially theocratic areas of countries including Sudan and Malaysia. Iran's and Pakistan's full banking systems follow Islamic law.

Because Islamic banks have dealings with international banks not based on the same principles, questions arise as to which rules international business transactions should follow. As Islamic banks are established in more countries, this concern decreases because Islamic banks can deal

MICROCREDIT IN TIBET

A microcredit bank makes small loans to people who have limited to no loan history. In April 2010, the Tibet Yurong Microcredit Company was established in Lhasa, Tibet. The capital for the company, more than $7 million, was provided by private investments. The company will cater to small and mid-sized companies, farmers, and herdsmen in the country.

Islamic banks have opened in many countries. Iran's national bank has a branch in the United Arab Emirates.

internationally with one another and avoid having to deal with a secular bank that charges interest.

Tithing and Gifts

In addition to redistributing resources and morality, one element common to most theocratic economies is the mandate to give money to the religion. In the early Mormon theocracy, each member was required to tithe, or give to the church, a portion of his or her income. Although there is no Mormon theocracy today, Mormons worldwide continue to follow the religious edict, tithing ten percent of their income to the church. These funds enrich the church and are also used to aid the poor and those in need.

In the Islamic Republic of Iran, as well as in Pakistan and many other Muslim countries, *zakat,* Islam's tax on wealth, is mandated. Zakat is considered to be one of the Five Pillars of Islam and is required of most Muslims. The tax is taken from food grains, fruit, livestock, gold and silver, and other goods.

RUMORS OF VATICAN WEALTH

Over the centuries, the Vatican has amassed significant wealth and has long been the subject of speculation by a public wanting to understand more about the theocracy's wealth. In the 1970s, the Vatican allowed reporters to investigate its financial holdings. The results of a long study revealed that rumors of Vatican riches were wildly inflated. Egidio Cardinal Vagnozzi, head of the Vatican's Prefecture for Economic Affairs at the time, estimated the wealth of the Vatican at approximately $500 million, excluding individual dioceses, which are each responsible for their own economic affairs.

These funds are given to the poor, to volunteers for jihad, and to others.

The world's longest-running theocracy, the Vatican, similarly depends on charitable donations by members of the Catholic Church. Today, these donations are voluntary and not required by the theocracy. But the Vatican dates back to the Middle Ages, and it did collect required taxes for the church at other times in its history. ⌘

9

Overlap with Other Forms of Government

Scholars have divergent views on the definition and degrees of theocracy in relation to other systems of government. In *The Political Economy in Theocracy*, editors Mario Ferrero and Ronald Wintrobe summarize,

> *What is a theocracy? In its literal meaning, theocracy is rule by God. But of course God does not rule directly, and here the definitions diverge. A workable definition that takes the*

middle ground is "a government grounded and constrained by religious theology."[1]

But where does religious influence end and theocracy begin? The answer is not always clear.

Some scholars have defined what they call a secular theocracy, in which the priestly class and sacred texts do not derive from religion but function in the same way as their religious counterparts. Such governments include the former Communist countries in which communism formed an overarching principle or ideology that informed all aspects of society. Schools taught this body of thought in the same way that religion is taught in schools in a theocracy.

Other thinkers see little difference between theocracy and dictatorship. This is a form of government in which one leader has absolute power and rule over culture, society, and politics. Dictators throughout history have included Adolf Hitler, who ruled Germany from 1933 to 1945, and Benito Mussolini, dictator of Italy from 1922 to 1943. Dictators

> "The theocratic form of government is particularly difficult to understand, partly because the word can be taken to mean so many different things and also because the regimes which can be labeled theocratic in one sense or another appear so different."[2]
>
> —*Mario Ferrero and Ronald Wintrobe,* The Political Economy in Theocracy

lead authoritarian governments, meaning that citizens must submit to their rule and dictates in all areas of their lives. Some theocracies function as dictatorships with religious law serving as absolute authority.

In the totalitarian country of North Korea, the personality cults built around the ruling Kim family have produced a close resemblance to a state religion without an actual religious doctrine. Kim Il Sung, who ruled from 1948 to 1994, and his son Kim Jong Il, who has been North Korea's leader since 1994, are viewed as omniscient and godlike by the country's citizens.

Theocracy can take different forms and cannot be solely related to any single form of government. Historically, theocracies have overlapped with monarchies, dictatorships, and even democracies. Not all theocratic governments force their beliefs on their citizens, but this is common.

Democracy and Theocracy

Democracy's belief in individual freedoms and independence of thought and action is in direct conflict with theocracy's demand that religion govern individual, social, and political life. One interesting case study for the relationship between democracy and theocracy can be found in Israel. Founded in 1948 as a homeland for Jews, Israel sits on a strip of land between Egypt and Jordan, land considered sacred to practitioners of three major world religions: Judaism, Islam, and Christianity.

Israel began as a place for all Jews, from the secular to the ultraorthodox. A secular democracy, led by an elected prime minister, has governed Israel since its earliest days. Israel does not have a constitution or a bill of rights; the Knesset, or Israeli parliament, creates legislation in the country.

Since its inception, the Israeli government has adopted laws that reflect Orthodox Jewish rules regarding marriage, adoption, and divorce; the necessity to serve kosher food in public; forbidding of the Israeli national airline to fly on the Sabbath; and releasing Orthodox Jews from compulsory military service with the understanding that prayer will serve as a substitute. Even Jews who do not practice the conservative Jewish Orthodoxy, and cultural Jews who do not practice the religion at all, must follow Orthodox law in these areas. For nearly 50 years, this situation remained in

ASSASSINATION BY A FUNDAMENTALIST

In 1994, Israeli Prime Minister Yitzak Rabin was awarded the Nobel Peace Prize (along with Yasser Arafat and Shimon Peres) for his work for peace between Israelis and Palestinians. Rabin had offered the Palestinians limited self-rule in Gaza and parts of the West Bank, angering Orthodox Jews who believed Jewish settlers should remain in the disputed areas. On November 4, 1995, Rabin was assassinated, not by a Palestinian, but by a fundamentalist Jewish Israeli who opposed the prime minister's attempts to offer West Bank lands to Palestinians.

Israel without significant problems between Jewish groups. But since the early twenty-first century, Orthodox Jews have begun to demand control over more areas. In response, other Israeli citizens have begun to question the concessions made to the Orthodox—approximately 16 percent of Israel's population—for so many years.

Ultraorthodox factions challenge individual freedoms of Israeli citizens. In the city of Jerusalem, women have been stoned for not dressing in what some Orthodox Jews deem appropriate. Men have been attacked for driving in Orthodox neighborhoods on the Sabbath. Theocracy in the form of fundamentalist Jewish sects in Israel continues to prove challenging to Israel's young democracy.

RADICAL IDEAS IN ISRAEL

New York–born rabbi Meir Kahane moved to Israel and preached a fundamentalist Judaism that disallows all Arabs in Israel. His movement, Kach, is still alive in Israel. An Arab assassin killed Kahane in 1990, but his ideas remain influential in some parts of Israel. In particular, they fuel the Hilltop Youth, a radical Jewish settler group, in the Gaza strip.

Monarchy and Theocracy

In the course of its history, Saudi Arabia has had a strong relationship between theocracy and monarchy. Saudi Arabia is governed by a monarchy

*King Faisal ruled Saudi Arabia
from 1964 to 1975.*

that dates back to the eighteenth century, when the family of Muhammad Ibn Saud ruled much of the Arabian Peninsula for approximately 150 years. In 1932, Abd Al Aziz Al Saud, a direct descendent of Ibn Saud, established what is now the Kingdom of Saudi Arabia, with himself as the monarch.

Yet, Saudi Arabia has also been home to Islam, dating back to the seventh century, when the prophet Muhammad was born and established the first holy sites in the Arabian Desert there. When Ibn Saud made himself the monarch, he also designated the Koran as the nation's constitution. The House of Saud constitutes a royal lineage, and only members of this family are eligible to hold the throne. Unlike the Islamic Republic of Iran, where religious leaders hold a higher position than the elected president, the king is the ruler of Saudi Arabia. However, the monarch must still follow Sharia, and its strict interpretation still dictates daily life in the country.

While religious authorities do not rule in the country, they still have tremendous

ENGLISH MONARCHY AND THE CHURCH

Historically, European monarchs have been closely associated with the clergy. In the sixteenth century, the young King Henry VIII of England worked closely with Thomas Wolsey, a minister and, later, a cardinal in the Catholic Church. Wolsey amassed significant power in the royal court. When Henry fell in love with Anne Boleyn and wanted a divorce from his current wife so he could marry her, Wolsey beseeched the pope on the king's behalf and failed. He was fired and arrested. Henry VIII convinced the archbishop to grant him an annulment. The pope was furious. A feud ensued over who had authority, the king or the pope, ending in a legendary breach between the Vatican and the English monarchy.

power, particularly in the areas of society and education. The monarchy works with religious leaders, granting funds to further their goals of establishing a society more reliant on Sharia. The ulema, or scholarly religious men, provide guidance to the royal family. While religious leaders also perform ceremonial functions, rituals, and sometimes administrative or legislative roles in a monarchy, they do not define governmental leadership.

Saudi Arabia has no political parties and does not hold elections. Unlike Israel, founded on the basis that all Jewish people would be welcome, Saudi Arabia allows only a single version of Islam, a puritanical form of fundamentalist Islam called Wahhabism. Strict Sharia, enforced by the state, forbids dancing, tobacco, and alcohol. Men and women are segregated at school and work. Women must wear the full burka everywhere, unless there are designated women-only areas where they are allowed to remove their veil. Women's jobs are limited to education and medicine.

In the 1930s, Saudi Arabia was found to have massive amounts of oil. Today, the country is the world's foremost producer and exporter of oil and generates huge profits from oil each year. These funds have increased the standard of living for all Saudi Arabians; they pay no taxes and receive free education and health care. However, those living in the monarchy must abide by strict codes of behavior dictated by Sharia.

Theocracy, Democracy, and Tribal Rule

In contrast to Saudi Arabia, Afghanistan, which is a democratic country, is one of the world's poorest countries. It ranks 181 out of 182 nations in human development—an index that rates the overall well-being of a nation—and the vast majority of Afghanis, approximately 72 percent, are illiterate.[3] Afghanistan's terrain is rocky and mountainous, making government centralization geographically challenging. In addition, the official government has less power than tribes. The struggle between religious tribal clerics and government has occurred over the past century, through Afghanistan's monarchy, occupation, and fragile democracy.

During the nineteenth century, England and Russia fought for control of the land, but in 1919, Afghanistan became an independent nation ruled by King Ammanullah Khan, who named himself king in 1926. The king attempted to modernize the young country with reforms including coeducational schools. But religious tribal clerics rejected the reforms, and the king was overthrown in 1929. A successor, Zahir Shah, reigned on the Afghani throne for 40 years, during which rivalries escalated between the government and Islamic revolutionaries and tribes fighting against modernization.

In 1973, King Zahir Shah was overthrown by his former prime minister, Mohammed Daoud. In 1978, Communist factions overthrew Daoud and tried to institute a Soviet-modeled state, spurring rebellions across the country. In 1979, Soviet troops entered Afghanistan to provide assistance for the new regime, and the Afghani mujahideen, or Muslim freedom fighters, continued to rebel. The United States joined the conflict to prevent the spread of Soviet influence and communism and contributed, along with other Western nations, weapons and training for the mujahideen.

The Soviets finally withdrew in 1989, and a civil war arose between competing Afghani factions. It's estimated that more than 1 million Afghanis lost their lives during the war, and an estimated 1 million more fled as refugees. In 1994, the religious leader Mullah Mohammed Omar in Kandahar was able to organize local mujahideen and students against the warlords, forming the Taliban as a way to restore order to Afghanistan. The Taliban grew in strength and power. In 1997, the group renamed the country the Islamic Emirate of Afghanistan, and by 1998, the Taliban controlled most of the country.

In September 2001, militant Muslim revolutionaries attacked the United States. The mastermind of the attacks, Osama bin Laden, a militant fundamentalist Muslim and a leader of al-Qaeda, had been given refuge by the Taliban and was living in Afghanistan at the time of the attacks. After the tragedy of September 11, the US Army entered Afghanistan and toppled the theocratic Taliban regime in the cities. As of 2010, the official leader of the government is President Hamid Karzai, who won a widely observed and much debated election in 2009. However,

Members of the Islamic fundamentalist group al-Qaeda attacked the democratic United States on September 11, 2001.

Afghanistan remains in the grip of struggle between fundamentalist Islam and democratic secularization and continues to suffer from deep poverty. ⌘

Human Rights and International Relations

Historically, there has been a divide between theocracy and human rights. If people are made to follow strict religious law, voluntary participation and choice are out of the question. A gap exists between the enforcement of strict religious laws and the humanistic International Bill of Rights, which guarantees safety, security, and liberty of mind and body to all.

The UN adopted the Universal Declaration of Human Rights on December 10, 1948. Fifty-eight

In 2010, an activist participated in a demonstration against the stoning of an Iranian woman convicted of adultery.

member states worked together to create the document. It is composed of 30 articles that define the rights of all people around the world and remains the international standard for how people should be treated and what they deserve. The document states that the dignity and equal rights of "all members of the human family is the foundation of freedom, justice and peace in the world," and pledges that the UN

> shall strive by teaching and education to promote respect for these rights and freedoms and by progressive measures, national and international, to secure their universal and effective recognition and observance, both among the peoples of Member States themselves and among the peoples of territories under their jurisdiction.[1]

At times, religious laws that govern theocratic nations and theocratic aspects of society conflict with the code of ethics defined in the Universal Declaration of Human Rights. For example, Article 16 states,

> Men and women of full age, without any limitation due to race, nationality or religion, have the right to marry and to found a family. They are entitled to equal rights as to marriage, during marriage and at its dissolution.[2]

This article conflicts with the marriage and divorce aspects of Sharia, which governs in Iran, Saudi Arabia, and parts of other nations in the Middle East and Africa. It also conflicts with Orthodox Jewish laws, which strictly govern marriage and divorce in Israel. In instituting theocratic law regarding marriage and family, these nations go against internationally agreed-upon human rights. In response, the international community speaks out against the human rights abuses and has used methods including economic sanctions, protests, petitions, and even military force.

Interpreting Secular and Religious Law

Since it was founded in 1979, the Islamic Republic of Iran has had a contentious relationship with the international community. This has derived from conflicts between religious and secular law, human rights violations, and political and economic differences.

> "All human beings are born free and equal in dignity and rights. They are endowed with reason and conscience and should act towards one another in a spirit of brotherhood."[3]
>
> —*Universal Declaration of Human Rights, Article 1*

One particular source of conflict between the Islamic Republic of Iran and the international community has been in the nation's treatment of its citizens. Human rights groups, including the internationally recognized independent nonprofit Human Rights Watch, have protested Iran's treatment of women, forms of punishment, and policing of citizens.

The primary response from the United States and other western nations has been to impose economic sanctions. As recently as September 2010, the United States implemented sanctions against the Islamic Republic of Iran. The sanctions prohibit US citizens from engaging in business with Iranian officials known to have taken part in human rights abuses. Of the sanctions, Secretary of State Hillary Clinton said,

On these officials' watch or under their command Iranian citizens have been arbitrarily beaten, tortured, raped, black-mailed, and killed. Yet the Iranian government has ignored repeated calls from the international community to end these abuses, to hold to account those responsible, and respect the rights and fundamental freedoms of its citizens.[4]

Article 5 of the Universal Declaration of Human Rights states, "No one shall be subjected to torture or to cruel, inhuman or degrading treatment or punishment."[5] While many in the international community see stoning, a legal punishment in

"Islam is not a new religion, but the same truth that God revealed through all His prophets to every people. For a fifth of the world's population, Islam is both a religion and a complete way of life. Muslims follow a religion of peace, mercy, and forgiveness, and the majority have nothing to do with the extremely grave events which have come to be associated with their faith."[6]

—The Islamic Affairs Department, the Embassy of Saudi Arabia, Washington DC

In September 2010, US Secretary of State Hillary Clinton announced sanctions against Iran for its human rights abuses.

Iran (and in some other Muslim nations) as cruel and inhuman, the Iranian government interprets it as acceptable under Islamic law.

In July 2010, a woman was sentenced to execution by stoning in the Islamic Republic of Iran. Writing about the incident, the Associated Press explained,

> In the Muslim world, stoning is a relatively rare means of punishing those who commit adultery (zina al-mohsena) under Islamic Law. It is considered a form of community justice and has its fair share of critics both among human rights groups and Islamic clerics. Those sentenced to stoning, or "lapidation" as it is also called, are buried in a hole and covered with soil (men up to their waists; women to a line above their breasts), according to Article 102 of the Islamic Penal Code. A selected group then executes the alleged adulterers using rocks and sticks.[7]

According to the news agency, death by stoning derives from ancient Greece and from Judeo-Christian religious texts and is cited in the Old Testament of the Bible but is not mentioned in the Koran.

Although rare and disapproved of by some Islamic clerics and by secular law, Iranian legislature sees its role in meting out this sentence as fulfilling Islamic law. Despite protests from the international community, including citizen protests and statements against stoning from world leaders including the president of the European Union and representatives of the Vatican, death by stoning also remains legal not only in the Islamic Republic of Iran but also in Afghanistan and Islamic sections of Nigeria, Pakistan, Sudan, and the United Arab Emirates.

Opponents point to additional mistreatments of women under religious law. In Muslim countries, women have an enforced dress code dictated by Sharia. While many religious women willingly abide by these laws, others, including more moderate or modernized Muslims in Muslim nations and around the world, find them to be in violation of women's rights as defined by the Universal Declaration of Human Rights. In Orthodox areas of Israel, women must also observe extreme modesty, including covering their hair and limbs and wearing long skirts.

Methods of protest against human rights have included economic and political sanctions and speaking out for human rights. A large number of independent nonprofit groups worldwide have spoken out to help women, girls, political prisoners, and other victims of human rights. But governmental responses to human rights abuses in Iran and in other nations have varied, depending on the political, cultural, and economic climate. Unlike nonprofit groups, such as Human Rights Watch, economic and security interests also play a role in how nations choose to respond to human rights abuses in Iran and other theocracies.

The United States, Saudi Arabia, and Afghanistan

The United States government's complicated relationships with the Saudi royal family and the Taliban of Afghanistan demonstrate the precarious balance between theocracy and other forms of government in the international community. Although governed by a monarchy, the Koran remains the Saudi constitution. Also, the House of Saud, the ruling family, makes cultural and political concessions to the nation's Islamic religious leaders. These include giving the clerics millions of dollars of Saudi oil wealth. Much of this money is used to spread Islam, often to poor parts of the world.

MODERATE MUSLIM KILLED

Ahmed Shah Massoud was a hero in the Afghan War against the Soviets. As the leader of the moderate Muslim Northern Alliance, Massoud fought side by side with the Taliban against the Soviet invasion. After the war, he remained a moderate leader in the north of Afghanistan, keeping that area of the country out of the hands of militants. Two days before the 9/11 terrorist attacks on the United States, Massoud was killed by a suicide bomber associated with al-Qaeda.

During the Soviet invasion of Afghanistan from 1979 to 1989, the United States financially supported Afghanistan to fight against the Soviets. Some of the money may have gone to schools that nurtured the development of the Taliban, the radical Islamic group that went on to transform Afghanistan into a theocracy after the Soviets left the country. US funds helped the Afghans fight off Soviet forces, but in the aftermath of the struggle, the most radical of these fighters, the Taliban under Mullah Omar, sheltered Osama bin Laden, the militant Saudi organizer of the 9/11 terrorist attacks on the United States. When al-Qaeda, led by bin Laden, claimed responsibility for the 9/11 attacks, bin Laden was still living in Afghanistan.

Oil wealth continues to complicate the situation. For almost a century, the United States was the biggest oil producer in the world and remains the biggest consumer, using 25 percent of the world's oil. Since the discovery of oil in Saudi Arabia in the 1930s, that nation has played a vital role in governing the price of oil, a value that deeply impacts that US economy. Friendship with Saudi Arabia is pivotal to US economic and security interests.

US GOVERNMENTAL PRESENCE IN SAUDI ARABIA

The United States established diplomatic relations with Saudi Arabia in 1933. The first US embassy opened there in 1944 in the city of Jeddah. A growing US presence in Saudi Arabia, in response to the production of oil, led to the establishment of the US consulate general in Dhahran in 1944. In 1984, the US Embassy moved to Riyadh, and the embassy in Jeddah became home to the US consulate general.

On the one hand, the United States is allied with Saudi Arabia. US President George W. Bush, president from 2001 to 2009 and whose family is involved in the oil business, was particularly friendly with the monarchy. But, on the other, the United States must work to prevent the spread of radical militant Islam, which threatens democracy and human rights. The monarchy openly opposes terror tactics, but 15 of the 19 hijackers in the 9/11 terror attacks hailed from Saudi Arabia. (Bin Laden was born in Saudi Arabia, but his citizenship had been revoked in 1994 due to his association with international acts of terror.) Nevertheless, the US friendship with Saudi Arabia remains integral to diplomatic and economic relations. According to the US Department of State,

> Saudi Arabia's unique role in the Arab and Islamic worlds, its possession of the world's largest reserves of oil, and its strategic location make its friendship important to the United States. [8]

The Growth of Islamic Fundamentalism

Over the past three decades, religious fundamentalism, predominantly Islam, but also Christian, Jewish, and Hindu, has been on the rise in areas all across the globe. Religious scholar Karen Armstrong attributes this to growing fears of modernization, as well as to the spread of Western morals and capitalism in urban areas, a situation that has left many rural and poor people out of the process. In the introduction to her 2001 book, *The Battle for God*, Armstrong wrote,

> We shall find that modernization has led to a polarization of society, but sometimes, to prevent an escalation of the conflict, we must

try to understand the pain and perceptions of the other side. Those of us—myself included— who relish the freedoms and achievements of modernity find it hard to comprehend the distress these cause religious fundamentalists. Yet modernization is often experienced not as a liberation but as an aggressive assault.[9]

Despite the reasons, this increase in religious fundamentalism lies in direct conflict with secular law, human rights, and democracy. While religious leaders see modernization as a threat to their ways of life, many other people see religious fundamentalism as hazardous to individual freedoms and societal advancement.

Some countries that have faced the dilemma head-on include Afghanistan, where a weak central democracy continues to fight against religious extremists; Turkey, where modernization by the secular government has led to backlash by Islamic fundamentalists; and Pakistan, established in 1947 as a religiously Muslim but democratically governed country. In Pakistan, Muslims share a tenuous coexistence with Hindus. Moderate interpretations of both religions struggle with fundamentalist edicts by extremists.

Egypt, home to an ancient theocracy, is governed today by a military-backed secular democracy. For many years, there was a single political party in Egypt, the National Democratic Party, and its candidates ran unopposed. This situation bred resentment that led to the formation, in 1928, of the Muslim Brotherhood. Founder Hasan al-Banna advocated a fundamentalist version of Islam, and the organization approved violence against nonbelievers. Today, the Muslim Brotherhood appeals to citizens by providing education, welfare, and health care, but it is also involved in acts of terror.

Fundamentalist groups have launched attacks on visitors to Egypt. Tourists travel from all over the world to see the pyramids, temples, and mummies from the ancient Egyptian civilization. From 1992 to 1997, and again between 2004 and 2006, Islamic fundamentalists who wanted to strike out against the secular Egyptian government launched attacks that killed dozens of citizens of Europe, Israel, and the United States.

ASSASSINATION OF A MODERATE EGYPTIAN PRESIDENT

Egyptian President Anwar el-Sadat worked for a peaceful solution to his nation's conflicts with neighboring Israel. In 1977, he proposed an open dialogue with Israel, prompting angered responses from religious extremists. On October 6, 1981, Islamic extremists assassinated President Sadat while he sat watching a military parade.

In 2005, in response to growing pressure from diverse factions, including Islamic fundamentalists, to hold more open elections, the government of Egypt under President Hosni Mubarak amended the Egyptian constitution to allow for multiparty elections. Later that year, Mubarak easily won the election.

Militant Islam and International Terrorism

On September 11, 2001, the United States experienced the horror of terrorism at the hands of Islamic extremists led by Osama bin Laden, a member of al-Qaeda. Hijackers took over four US airplanes full of civilians and flew them into designated targets on US soil. Two planes hit the World Trade Center in New York City, and a third plane flew into the Pentagon in Washington DC. The fourth plane crashed in a field in Pennsylvania, killing everyone on board but missing its target, presumed to be the White House. In the fiery crashes, 2,752 people were killed.[10]

September 11 was a deep tragedy for the United States and the world, but sadly, the United States was not the first or last nation to experience violent attacks by Islamic extremists. Egyptian tourists have suffered from violent attacks for nearly two decades. In November 2008, Islamic terrorists attacked sites in Mumbai, India, terrorizing citizens for three days and killing 174 people.[11] In July 2010, people watching the World Cup in Uganda were killed in a bomb blast planted by militant Islamic fundamentalists.

Brendan O'Leary, author and professor of political science at the University of Pennsylvania, wrote,

> *Beginning in the early 1970s, Islamic militants revolted against incumbent regimes in Muslim majority countries, and exacerbated major conflicts in Algeria, Egypt, Sudan, Palestine, Lebanon, Afghanistan, Pakistan, Iraq, and*

People mourned the loss of those killed in the Mumbai terrorist attack of 2008.

Malaysia to name just a few sites of attempted jihad. They revolted in the name of their religion and with the goal of establishing an Islamic state, sometimes described, notably by Osama bin Laden, as the restoration of the caliphate.[12]

This instability in individual nations soon bled onto the world stage in the form of international terrorism, creating a climate of uncertainty and insecurity in the world.

As of 2010, the religion that poses the greatest risk to security and democracy is radical Islam, but danger is not housed in one religion or set of beliefs. It depends on the religion and its interpretation by leaders. ⌘

Theocracy and the United States

O ne of the founding tenets of the United States of America is the freedom of religion. In leaving England, the early settlers wanted the freedom to practice whatever form of religion they chose. But the religious atmosphere was not as varied as it is in the country today. The vast majority of early American governors, leaders, and founders of the United States were Protestant. In granting freedom of religion, they were presumably addressing the freedoms they lacked in England and most likely had not envisioned the multiplicity of religions that

The US Constitution

would one day be practiced in the country they helped to found.

Religion in Early America

Protestantism is a Christian religion that grew out of the Reformation, a moral and philosophical protest against the Catholic Church that began with the writings of Martin Luther in 1517. Since that time, many forms of Protestantism, including Calvinism practiced by the Puritans, arose in Europe and then in the American colonies.

In the colonies, religion was a primary issue. The Puritans' Massachusetts Bay Colony, established in 1630, was effectively the first theocracy in the new territory. Other colonies related to religion in different ways. Roger Williams, ousted from the Massachusetts Bay Colony for his religious views, purchased land and founded the colony of Providence, so named in thanks to God. His colony maintained a tolerant approach to religion, accepting settlers of all religious persuasions. The colony's charter, written in 1663, stated, "[The] flourishing civil state may stand and best be maintained with full liberty in religious concernments."[1] Williams's colony later became the state of Rhode Island.

The United States Constitution, signed in 1776, guarantees the freedom of religion and effectively creates a divide between church and the state. This separation remains firmly in place, but it has been challenged in various ways throughout the country's history.

A Mormon Theocracy

In the early years of the United States, the nation included only a portion of what are now the 50 states. Vast areas in the middle of the country and on the West Coast were territories not yet claimed by the United States. In the midst of these, a young theocracy based on the Mormon religion grew and flourished. The Mormon Church, officially called the Church of Jesus Christ of Latter-Day Saints, began in the 1820s when Joseph Smith had a series of angelic visions. Among these was an angel named Moroni, who showed the young man a series of golden plates. Returning to the spot the next day, Smith is said to have found the plates and, through a laborious process, transcribed their contents to create the Book of Mormon, which was published in 1830.

"Congress shall make no law respecting an establishment of religion, or prohibiting the free exercise thereof; or abridging the freedom of speech, or of the press; or the right of the people peaceably to assemble, and to petition the government for a redress of grievances."[2]

—*First Amendment of the US Constitution*

With the help of its charismatic leader, the new religion spread quickly. Although it is a version of Christianity, it was radically different from the Protestantism practiced by most settlers, and Smith was harshly criticized. With his new followers, Smith left his home in the area of New York and settled first in Kirtland, Ohio, and then in Independence, Missouri, near where Kansas City lies today.

From the start, Smith established himself as the ruler of both the church and the settlement. In the Doctrine of the Covenants of the Latter-Day Saints, one of the documents in which Smith transcribed his visions, he stated,

Wherefore, hear my voice and follow me, and you shall be a free people, and ye shall have no laws but my laws when I come, for I am your lawgiver, and what can stay my hand?[3]

MORMONISM GROWING

The Mormon religion is one of the fastest-growing religions in the United States. Mormons number approximately 14 million worldwide today.[4] The leader of a church is called president, but also prophet, seer, and revelator, and is seen to be in communication with God.

Relations between the Mormons and the local settlers were uneasy. Tensions erupted in 1838 when settlers in Missouri attacked a Mormon settlement, killing approximately 18 people, in what is known as Huan's Mill Massacre. This prompted Smith to move his community again. They settled at Nauvoo, Illinois, where they built a militia to ward off potential attackers.

Throughout this period, Smith continued to have visions and make prophecies. In 1843, he gave the prophecy of plural marriage, citing a commandment from God that justified Mormon men taking multiple wives. This practice was at odds with the cultural mores of the Protestant settlers and with Illinois law. Smith was jailed for inciting riot and declaring martial law, and an angry mob broke into the jail holding Smith and killed him and another man.

"America has long been felt by Europeans to take God too seriously."[5]

—Brendan O'Leary, essayist in The Political Economy of Theocracy

Before his death, Smith had built the Mormon settlement into a thriving community of approximately 15,000, with himself as the religious and governmental head. When he died, he had not yet named a successor. A new leader emerged in Brigham Young, who led the Mormons into the US territory of Utah. Young controlled the territory in Utah as the head of the church, the legislature, and the government. Young, too, believed in plural marriage, though it was against US law, and is reported to have had between 30 and 50 wives.

The practice of polygamy was at odds with the secular government of the United States, which the Mormons saw as illegitimate. Tensions rose between Mormons and non-Mormons, and

A wood engraving of Brigham Young, 1854

in 1857, a militia of Mormon extremists attacked a wagon train headed to California, killing approximately 120 people.

The practice of polygamy kept Utah from statehood for many years. In 1890, the Mormon Church officially denounced polygamy. Less than a decade later, in 1896, Utah was admitted as a state, thereby ending the theocracy in Utah.

The Rise of Christian Fundamentalism

The past four decades have seen a rise in fundamentalist religious views all over the world. Religious scholar and author Karen Armstrong attributes this to a reaction to growing secularization and modernization. On the world stage, militant Islamic extremists have headlined this battle, but in the United States, it is often fundamentalist Christians who have clashed against the secular legislature and the government in many aspects of society.

Fundamentalist Christianity, commonly referred to as the religious right for its conservative moral and political views, is not new to the United States. In his bestselling book *American Theocracy*, Kevin Phillips writes, "Christianity in the United States, especially Protestantism, has always had an evangelical—which is to say missionary—and frequently a radical or combative streak." Phillips continues, "No other contemporary Western nation shares this religious intensity and its concomitant proclamation that Americans are God's chosen people and nation."[6]

Fundamentalist Christians express their fervor in a social, political, and economic agenda based on their interpretation of the Bible. Leaders aim to effect change through politics, speeches, and the introduction of legislation. At the same time, some individuals act out their religious beliefs in radical and violent ways.

One primary example can be found in fundamentalist Christians' radical stance against abortion, which is legal in the majority of US states. Long the topic of debate among politicians, the issue of abortion has also incited individual acts of violence against abortion providers. The first of these occurred in Pensacola, Florida, in 1993, when a religious radical shot and killed Dr. David Gunn. This event led to a string of violent acts against abortion providers, perpetrated in the name of religion.

The most recent iteration of Christian fundamentalism in the United States is a radical militant movement called Reconstructionism. This distinctly theocratic ideology calls for replacing the secular Constitution with Old Testament Biblical law. As Armstrong and other scholars have noted, Reconstructionist ideas share much in common with radical Islam, including severely restrictive views toward women and family life, harsh punishments including death by stoning, and the justification

LOBBYING FOR CHRISTIAN LEGISLATION

From 1979 to 1989, the US political action group Moral Majority, founded by the Reverend Jerry Falwell and made up of conservative, fundamentalist Christians, lobbied for legislation sympathetic to their religious beliefs, including support of prayer in schools and opposition to the Equal Rights Amendment—a proposed amendment to the US Constitution that was designed to ensure that all rights granted by law are applied equally to men and women.

of violence in the name of religious beliefs. Reconstructionists constitute a small minority of the religious right.

Just as there are many Muslims who hold moderate religious beliefs, the majority of Christians are not fundamentalist. Also, fundamentalists (of any faith) are not necessarily violent. Nonetheless, violence has been one of many tactics used by groups of fundamentalist Christians in the United States to assert a religiously radical agenda.

Fundamentalist Religion and Secular Education

The battle for women's reproductive rights is only one area of society that has witnessed the struggle between fundamentalist Christians and more moderate Christians and secular Americans. Another area affected by this strife, though less violently, is education.

What children learn, and how they learn it, is central to the functioning of a society. For this reason, members of the religious right have waged legislative battles to change curricula to fit their perspective. Court battles have centered on what can and cannot be taught in schools sponsored by government funds, with theological beliefs playing a central role in these lawsuits. Despite the United States not being a theocracy, fundamentalist Christian lobbying has impacted curriculum in Kentucky, Mississippi, Texas, and other states.

As recently as 2010, the State Board of Education in Texas adopted controversial new curriculum standards that some see as moving public schools in a theocratic direction. One of these includes using textbooks that include creationism and do not include the doctrine of separation of church and state that is protected in the Constitution. Texas school board member Don McLeroy stated, "We need to have students compare and contrast this current view of separation of church and state with the actual language in the First Amendment," while school board member Mavis Knight called the board's decision a "travesty."[7] Knight took issue with the new standard, stating that it "implies there is no such thing as the legal doctrine of separation of church and state."[8]

Another target of Christian fundamentalists has been the science curriculum, in particular, the teaching of evolution, which they see as contradictory to theological beliefs about creation. The long history of this battle was recently revived in relation to global warming.

THE TEA PARTY MOVEMENT

The Tea Party Movement is a sociopolitical movement that grew out of a grassroots political organization to raise funds to oppose the election of President Barack Obama. Since 2009, it has grown into a national conservative movement that seeks to influence legislation and elections in favor of its conservative agenda.

In the summer of 2010, Kentucky legislators introduced a bill that would encourage students to examine the accuracy of theories such as evolution and global warming. Similar bills have been passed in Texas, Louisiana, and Oklahoma. This suggests that linking global warming with evolution allows legislators to avoid the charge of trying to breach the divide of church and state that evolution addresses. When fundamentalists have focused their educational reform strategy on creationism, which directly conflicts with the science of evolution, popular opinion has tended to be against them. But when fundamentalist Christian efforts at education reforms were connected to examining the validity of global warming, which more Americans question than evolution (despite scientists having proven its accuracy), their efforts were more successful.

Can the United States Become a Theocracy?

During the presidency of George W. Bush, the US government moved in an increasingly religious direction. In addition to making numerous references connecting his leadership to his Christian faith, President Bush signed a controversial executive order in 2001 establishing a federal Department of Faith, which oversaw the allocation of taxpayers' dollars to religious organizations. Since the United States has a legal separation of church and state, a governmental official establishing a religious institution goes against US law.

This swing between conservative and liberal perspectives on religion is part of the history of the nation. Journalist and author Frederick Clarkson wrote in *Eternal Hostility*,

> *From the persecution of Quakers, Jesuits, and "witches" in the Massachusetts Bay Colony during the 1600s throughout the bitter Presidential Campaign of 1800, and the advent of the Christian Right in the 1980s, an animating, underlying theme of the American experience has been the struggle between democratic and theocratic values.*[9]

Despite the constitutional divide between church and state, this struggle continues. But will it continue to swing back and forth within the context of the secular constitution, or could it reach a tipping point and move the country toward a theocracy? One vital concern of Americans who oppose or fear theocracy has been the Supreme Court, the highest court in the country, which is capable of making legal decisions that effect constitutional changes. Judges are bound to rule in a nonpartisan way, but they interpret the law and Constitution according to their understanding and worldview. A majority of fundamentalist Christian judges could potentially tip the balance toward theocracy, but this is unlikely given numerous checks and balances in the democratic system.

Religious scholar Karen Armstrong suggests that there is an increasing need to balance what she calls mythos—poetry, spirituality, and religion—with logos—science, intellect, and technology. In the United States and around the world, the rise of fundamentalism points to a dissonance between mythos and logos, and between religious and secular law, specifically in relation to individual freedoms and human rights. This balance will affect the possibility of future theocracies. The challenge for US leaders and other leaders of free nations is to maintain justice and security while allowing people to believe and practice different religions or no religion at all. ⌘

Quick Facts

Definition of Theocracy

The word *theocracy* comes from the Greek words for "god," *theos*, and "power," *kratos*. Theocracy is a form of government in which power is designated as coming from the divine. Every aspect of a theocratic government is informed and determined by religious beliefs and law, as interpreted by a leader understood to have a special connection to the divine. A theocracy can exist under any form of religion and anywhere in the world. It is a rare form of government.

Well-Known Theocratic States

- Islamic Republic of Iran
- The Vatican

Organization of Theocratic Government

Theocracies are organized differently, depending on the state religion and the degree to which the leaders interpret it. The majority of theocracies are led by one supreme leader who has jurisdiction over religious, civic, and legislative matters and is supported by a strong police or military that enforces the governmental edicts and laws.

Main Leadership Position

In all theocracies, the leader is considered to be a messenger of the divine. The leader is appointed or chosen by a god or gods and is responsible for interpreting the will of the divine in governance over social, cultural, and political life.

Founders and Advocates

The term *theocracy* is attributed to Flavius Josephus, a Jewish priest best known as the historian of the Jewish wars during the Roman Empire. He defined theocracy in contrast to the Greek classifications of democracy, aristocracy, and monarchy. He described the ancient Hebrew civilization as a theocracy ruled by God.

The Vatican, a Catholic theocracy, is the longest-running theocracy in history. It began in the seventh century and still exists as of 2010. It has been led by a succession of popes.

Historic Leaders

Queen Hatshepsut is considered the most successful woman ruler of ancient Egypt and remains the only widely known female theocratic ruler.

Joseph Smith was the first prophet and founder of the Mormon religion. He led the first Mormon theocracy in the areas that are now Ohio and Illinois.

Ayatollah Khomeini was a religious cleric banned from his native Iran. He returned to the country and played an integral role in the revolution resulting in the founding of the Islamic Republic of Iran. He was the nation's supreme ruler during the first ten years.

How Power Shifts

One way in which power shifts in theocracy is through revolution, violent or peaceful, combined with conversion. This was the case in Iran during the 1970s.

Another way that power commonly shifts in a theocracy is through the election of a new leader by a small group of trusted advisers of the leader who has passed away. This is the case in the Vatican.

Economic Systems

There is no single economic system that is used with theocracy. For centuries, the Vatican has operated its own finances within the context of changing economies. It also has its own bank.

The most developed economic system in a theocracy is the system of Islamic economics used in many Muslim countries. The primary feature that distinguishes Islamic economics from capitalism is the elimination of interest. Islamic banks practice trade and offer loans but without the use of interest.

The Roles of Citizens

In most theocracies, citizens are bound by law to follow religious law and have limited participation in the government. Recently in Iran, hundreds of thousands of Iranians took part in protests against the theocratic elections and aimed at giving citizens more voice in government. Iranian women's groups promote a more just and humane interpretation of Islam.

Personal Freedoms and Rights

Most theocracies demand that citizens practice the state religion. The right to freedom of religion is rare in a theocracy. Independence in social and cultural matters depends on the state religion but is most often limited by religious dogma and enforced by state police. The lives of people in theocracies are heavily influenced by religious law and custom and are policed by state authorities. Obedience is demanded of both men and women in strict theocracies, but women in particular are bound by strict laws governing their personal and social behavior. Punishments for disagreement and dissension tend to be prevalent and harsh under theocracy.

Strengths of Theocracies

- Support art and architecture (as long as it glorifies a god or gods and supports religion)
- Support education (as long as it includes religious training)

Weaknesses of Theocracies

- Lack of religious and cultural tolerance
- Authoritarian
- Poor record on human rights

Glossary

ayatollah
A title of respect for a religious leader of Shiite Muslims; also, the title given to the religious ruler of Iran.

chador
A large cloth worn by Muslim women that acts as a veil and a shawl over the body and head.

charter
A contract or an official guarantee of rights or territory.

civic
Related to the people, community, or citizenry of a nation.

cleric
A religious leader.

commonwealth
A state or a political unit founded by a law or a treaty.

democracy
A form of government in which ultimate power resides with the people.

imam
A Muslim leader who followed the line of the fourth caliph, Ali, and was deemed to be appointed by Allah and a successor of the prophet Muhammad.

jihad
A holy war waged by Muslims to defend Islam; one's personal struggle in devotion to Islam.

market
An aspect of economic activity that involves the buying and selling of goods and the regulation of prices.

monarchy
A form of government led by a king or a queen.

monotheism
The religious belief in only one God.

mujahideen
Those who engage in holy war; they initially arose to fight the Soviet invasion of Afghanistan and consisted of devout and moderate Muslims.

pharaoh
The title given to a ruler in ancient Egypt.

polytheism
The belief in and worship of more than one god.

pope
The title given to the bishop of Rome and head of the Catholic Church; also, the sovereign leader of the Vatican.

secular
Not religious.

shah
Sovereign of Iran.

Sharia
A legal framework for Islam based on the Koran; Islamic law.

Shia
A branch of Islam that believes that only one of the first four caliphs, the fourth caliph, Ali, a relative of the prophet Muhammad, was the rightful successor of Islam.

state
A government or a political organization of people in a defined area or territory.

Sunni
A branch of Islam, the largest in the world, that believes in the rightful succession of the caliphs as leaders of Islam, as opposed to the succession of the Prophet's family.

Additional Resources

Selected Bibliography

Ferrero, Mario, and Ronald Wintrobe. *The Political Economy in Theocracy*. New York: St. Martin's, 2009. Print.

Marty, Martin E., and R. Scott Appleby, eds. *Fundamentalisms and the State: Remaking Polities, Economies, and Militance*. Chicago: Chicago UP, 1993. Print.

Phillips, Kevin. *American Theocracy*. New York: Viking, 2006. Print.

Further Readings

Armstrong, Karen. *The Battle for God*. New York: Ballantine, 2001. Print.

Perl, Lila. *Theocracy*. New York: Marshall Cavendish Benchmark, 2008. Print.

Satrapi, Marjane. *Persepolis: The Story of a Childhood*. New York: Pantheon, 2004. Print.

Web Links

To learn more about theocracies, visit ABDO Publishing Company online at **www.abdopublishing.com**. Web sites about theocracies are featured on our Book Links page. These links are routinely monitored and updated to provide the most current information available.

Places to Visit

Salt Lake Temple

50 West North Temple Street, Salt Lake City, UT 84150
801-240-2640
www.ldschurchtemples.com/saltlake
The largest of Mormon churches and the fourth one built in Utah. Mormonism was the basis of a theocracy in early America and is a growing religion worldwide.

Vatican Museums

Vatican City, Vatican
mv.vatican.va/3_EN/pages/MV_Home.html
The Vatican Museums are home to some of the most famous art and architecture in the world, including the Sistine Chapel and the Gallery of Tapestries.

Source Notes

Chapter 1. Theocracy in the New World

1. Perry Miller, ed. *The American Puritans: Their Prose and Poetry*. Garden City, NY: Anchor Books, 1956. *Google Book Search*. Web. 8 Oct. 2010.

2. Karen Armstrong. *The Battle for God*. New York: Ballantine, 2001. *New York Times Book Review*. New York Times Company, n.d. Web. 12 Nov. 2010.

3. "Bill of Rights." *Cornell University Law School*. Legal Information Institute, Cornell University Law School, n.d. Web. 8 Oct. 2010.

4. Lila Perl. *Theocracy*. New York: Marshall Cavendish Benchmark, 2008. Print. 131.

Chapter 2. Power Dynamics in Theocracies

1. "Ancient Aztec Government." *Aztec-History.com*. N.p., n.d. Web. 8 Oct. 2010.

2. "Person of the Year: Ayatullah Khomeini." *Time*. Time, Inc., 7 Jan. 1980. Web. 8 Oct. 2010.

3. "2009 Country Reports on Human Rights Practices - Saudi Arabia." *UNHCR*. United Nations High Commissioner for Refugees, 11 Mar. 2010. Web. 8 Oct. 2010.

4. Ibid.

Chapter 3. Theocracies in the Ancient World

None.

Chapter 4. The Islamic Republic of Iran

1. Mike Shuster. "The Origins of the Shia-Sunni Split." *NPR*. NPR, 12 Feb. 2007. Web. 8 Oct. 2010.

2. Ibid.

3. "Ayatollah Khomeini." *Iran Chamber Society*. Iran Chamber Society, n.d. Web. 8 Oct. 2010.

Chapter 5. The Vatican

1. John F Kennedy. "I Believe in an America Where the Separation of Church and State Is Absolute." Greater Houston Ministerial Association. 12 Sept. 1960. Address. *Beliefnet*. Beliefnet, n.d. Web. 8 Oct. 2010.

2. Michael K. Holleran. "Daily Life at the Vatican." *National Catholic Reporter* 27 Oct. 1995. *Bnet*. CBS Interactive, n.d. Web. 8 Oct. 2010.

3. Pope Benedict XVI. "Message of His Holiness Pope Benedict XVI: Easter 2010." Address. *The Holy See*. Libreria Editrice Vaticana, 2010. Web. 8 Oct. 2010.

4. Thomas C. Fox. "Vatican investigates US women religious leadership." *National Catholic Reporter*, The National Catholic Reporter Publishing Company, 14 Apr. 2009. Web. 8 Oct. 2010.

5. Catholic News Service. "L.A. Archdiocese Reaches Agreement with More Than 500 Abuse Claimants." *AmericanCatholic.org*. St. Anthony Messenger Press, n.d. Web. 8 Oct. 2010.

Chapter 6. Civic Life in a Theocracy

1. Martin E. Marty and R. Scott Appleby, eds. *Fundamentalisms and the State: Remaking Polities, Economies, and Militance*. Chicago: Chicago UP, 1993. Print. 113.

2. "Pakistan's Acid Attack Victims Pin Hope on New Laws." *Dawn.com*. The DAWN Media Group, 4 Jan. 2010. Web. 8 Oct. 2010.

3. Golnaz Esfandiari. "Iranian Women's Rights Activist Recounts Decision To Cast Off Hijab." *Rferl.org*. Radio Free Europe/Radio Liberty, 13 July 2010. Web. 8 Oct. 2010.

4. Chris Niles. "UNICEF-EC Programme Gives a Second Chance to a Would-Be Child Bride in India." *Unicef*. UNICEF, 20 Aug. 2010. Web. 8 Oct. 2010.

Chapter 7. Theocracy, Art, and Education

1. "The Sacred Congregation for Catholic Education: The Catholic School." *The Holy See*. Libreria Editrice Vaticana, 2010. Web. 8 Oct. 2010.

2. Mike Celizic. "Beyond the Veil: Lives of Women in Iran." *TODAY in Iran*. MSNBC.com, 13 Sept. 2007. Web. 8 Oct. 2010.

3. Jeffrey Goldberg. "Education of a Holy Warrior." *The New York Times Magazine*. The New York Times Company, 25 June 2000. Web. 8 Nov. 2010.

Chapter 8. Theocratic Economies

1. Martin E. Marty and R. Scott Appleby, eds. *Fundamentalisms and the State: Remaking Polities, Economies, and Militance*. Chicago: Chicago UP, 1993. Print. 305.

2. Ibid. 209–291.

3. Ibid. 292.

Chapter 9. Overlap with Other Forms of Government

1. Mario Ferrero and Ronald Wintrobe. *The Political Economy in Theocracy*. New York: St. Martin's, 2009. Print. 2.

2. Ibid. 1.

3. "Human Development Report 2009: Afghanistan." *Human Development Reports*. United Nations Development Programme, n.d. Web. 1 Oct. 2010.

Chapter 10. Human Rights and International Relations

1. "The Universal Declaration of Human Rights." *United Nations*. The United Nations, 10 Dec. 1948. Web. 8 Oct. 2010.

2. Ibid.

3. Ibid.

4. Elise Labott. "U.S. Adds More Sanctions Against Iran for Human Rights Abuses." *CNN*. Cable News Network, 29 Sept. 2010. Web. 8 Oct. 2010.

5. "The Universal Declaration of Human Rights." *United Nations*. The United Nations, 10 Dec. 1948. Web. 8 Oct. 2010.

6. "Understanding Islam and Muslims." *Islami City*. Islami City, n.d. Web. 8 Oct. 2010.

7. Msnbc.com staff. "Where Is Stoning Legal, and How Is It Done?" *MSNBC.com*. MSNBC.com, 8 July 2010. Web. 8 Oct. 2010.

8. "Background Note: Saudi Arabia." *U.S. Department of State*. U.S. Department of State, 5 Apr. 2010. Web. 8 Oct. 2010.

9. Karen Armstrong. *The Battle for God*. New York: Ballantine, 2001. Print. xviii.

10. "New York Reduces 9/11 Death Toll by 40." *CNN.US*. Cable News Network, 29 Oct. 2003. Web. 8 Oct. 2010.

11 "Surviving Mumbai Gunman Convicted." *BBC*. BBC, 3 May 2010. Web. 8 Oct. 2010.

12. Mario Ferrero and Ronald Wintrobe. *The Political Economy in Theocracy*. New York: St. Martin's, 2009. Print. 10.

Chapter 11. Theocracy and the United States

1. "Rhode Island: Religions." *City-Data.com*. N.p., n.d. Web. 8 Oct. 2010.

2. "First Amendment." *Cornell University Law School*. Legal Information Institute, Cornell University Law School, n.d. Web. 8 Oct. 2010.

3. Joseph Smith. *Doctrine of the Covenants of the Church of the Latter Day Saints*. Salt Lake City, UT: The Church of Jesus Christ of the Latter Day Saints, 1921. Print. 55–56.

4. Peggy Fletcher Stack. "Monson Urges Mormons to Serve Missions." *The Salt Lake Tribune*. The Salt Lake Tribune, 6 Oct. 2010. Web. 8 Oct. 2010.

5. Mario Ferrero and Ronald Wintrobe. *The Political Economy in Theocracy*. New York: St. Martin's, 2009. Print. 14.

6. Kevin Phillips. *American Theocracy*. New York: Viking, 2006. Print. 100.

7. Terrence Stutz. "Texas State Board of Education Approves New Curriculum Standards." *DallasNews.com*. The Dallas Morning News, Inc., 22 May 2010. Web. 8 Oct. 2010.

8. Ibid.

9. Frederick Clarkson. *Eternal Hostility: The Struggle Between Theocracy and Democracy*. Monroe, ME: Common Courage Press, 1997. Print. 4.

Index